KEN SCOTLAND

KEN SCOTLAND

THE AUTOBIOGRAPHY

POLARIS
PUBLISHING

First published in 2020 by

POLARIS PUBLISHING LTD
c/o Aberdein Considine
2nd Floor, Elder House
Multrees Walk
Edinburgh
EH1 3DX

www.polarispublishing.com

Distributed by

ARENA SPORT
An imprint of Birlinn Limited

Text copyright © Kenneth Scotland, 2020

ISBN: 9781913538033
eBook ISBN: 9781913538040

British Library Cataloguing-in-Publication Data
A catalogue record for this book is available on request from the British Library.

Designed and typeset by Polaris Publishing, Edinburgh

Printed in Great Britain by Clays Ltd, Elcograf S.p.A.

CONTENTS

I should like to thank Allan Massie and Peter Burns
most sincerely for their editorial advice and encouragement.

In memory of my parents who brought me into the world to be part of a favoured generation; to my dear wife, Doreen, who I was lucky to meet at age seventeen and who has been a constant pillar of strength for sixty-six years; to our three boys and their wives, Robin and Hilde, Iain and Deb, Alistair and Siw and to their children and grand-children and future generations of Scotlands.

FOREWORD

'The past is a foreign country; they do things differently there.'
The opening sentence of L P Hartley's novel, *The Go-Between*,
has become hackneyed, but only because it so often strikes one
as true. Certainly, the rugby world which Ken Scotland recalls in
his autobiography will seem like a journey through an unknown
land to those whose experience is limited to the modern
professional game, whether as players or followers. Those who
play and follow the amateur club game will find some things
familiar, much that isn't.

It is an unusual as well as fascinating book in other respects
also. Unlike many rugby memoirs it hasn't been ghosted; it is
Ken's words you read, his voice you hear. Then he gives as much
attention to his life and career outside the game as he does to
rugby itself. His account of childhood in Edinburgh and his
education at George Heriot's paints a picture of a very different
Scotland, one in which modesty, good manners and reticence
were characteristic virtues. Showing-off and displays of emotion

were frowned upon. Any Heriot's boy who celebrated the scoring of a try in today's exuberant fashion would have received a sharp reprimand, and probably dropped for the next school match. His was a decorous childhood and youth: family, school, church, games (cricket, tennis and golf as well as rugby) and seaside holidays. Readers old enough to have known the Scotland of the 1940s and 50s will find much to revive nostalgic memories; younger ones much to surprise them, much that may make them envious of the ordered world he grew up in.

It is of course his rugby career that will interest most readers. Since it's now more than half a century since his playing career ended, few under pensionable age will remember watching him, and since he is, as I've intimated, a modest man, those who never saw him play won't learn from his own words why he was not only widely and deeply admired but also revered.

Writing an article about him a few years ago, and aware of how memory can gild a picture, I began by asking: 'Can Ken Scotland really have been as good as I remember him being?' It's a fair question to ask about the heroes of our youth. Well, in Ken's case, there is one clear and compelling answer. In 1969 the Irish full-back Tom Kiernan, captain of the 1968 British and Irish Lions in South Africa, was asked on the occasion of his fiftieth cap for Ireland who was the greatest player he had played against. He immediately replied: 'Ken Scotland. It was an honour to be on the same field.'

Ken wasn't an imposing figure. He was slim and pale, 5ft 10in in height and weighing not much over eleven stone. One first heard of him as a schoolboy in a very successful Heriot's XV. He played fly-half there and his partnership with his friend Eddie McKeating at inside centre was spoken of with awe at rival schools. His first international brought him immediate and wider fame. It was in Paris in January 1957. He was selected at full-back, a position he had scarcely played in. Scotland won

6–0; he kicked a penalty and dropped a goal. He had perfect hands, what are sometimes called cricketer's hands, and indeed he was a good club cricketer capped once by Scotland. He kicked equally well with either foot, as few of even the best professionals do now. Indeed, I have often remarked that the only way you could tell which was naturally his stronger foot was that he kicked penalties and conversions right-footed. But, like England's Jonny Wilkinson forty or fifty years later, he was adept at dropping goals with either foot. He was a beautiful passer of the ball; indeed Arthur Smith, the great right-wing three-quarter who captained both Scotland and the Lions, called him the best passer of the ball he played with, this at a time when the ability to pass well was the first thing required of a mid-field back. If Ken wasn't quite the first attacking full-back, the frequency and timing of his incursions into the three-quarter line, usually between the outside centre and wing, set an example which would transform full-back play. Henceforth, the number fifteen was not seen only as the last line of defence.

He was doing his National Service when first capped for Scotland and the chapter on National Service may surprise younger readers, some of whom may not be aware that for fifteen years after the end of the Second World War young men at the age of eighteen were called up to serve in the Forces for two years. For some, this was a valuable experience, for some a waste of time, for sportsmen a splendid and usually enjoyable opportunity. Ken served in the Royal Corps of Signals, based in Catterick, and played rugby or cricket several times a week. The Signals won the Army Cup in his time and he also played for the Army. The National Service chapter shows just what 'a foreign country' Britain was then.

If there had then been a reward for the 'Breakthrough International Player of the Year' Ken would surely have won it in the 1956/57 season. However, he was brought down to earth with a savage bump. In the autumn of 1957 he went up to Cambridge University and in the Freshman's Trial match played what he says was the worst game of his life. Ken was what in cricket is called a touch player, and when such a player is out of touch he looks all at sea, worse than others with more modest talents. In those days, newspapers like *The Times* and *The Daily Telegraph* reported the Freshmen's Trials at Cambridge and Oxford at length, not surprisingly because there were usually several present and future internationalists in the University sides. So Ken's performance was not merely disappointing; it was a very public humiliation. Not surprisingly, it took some time for confidence and form to return. He lost his place in the international team too, and there were some ready to dismiss him as a one-season wonder. So recovery was a test of character. He was back in the Scotland team for the Calcutta Cup when Robin Chisholm dropped out injured, and for the next five seasons held his place unchallenged.

The 1959 British & Irish Lions tour of Australia and New Zealand may be regarded as the peak of his career. The tour was very long. The Lions played thirty-three matches, including six Tests (two in Australia and four in New Zealand). They played exhilarating rugby and it was the only time in Ken's career when there were no distractions from study or work. He played in five of the six Tests, four at full-back, one as a centre. Happily he kept a diary on tour, and reproduces much of it here. So it would be superfluous for me to anticipate his account. I would add only a couple of things. He is modest about his own part in the tour, and you wouldn't think he was hailed as one of the stars of the Lions' brilliant back division. His rival for the number fifteen jersey was Terry Davies. I remember Davies as a lovely player for Wales and Llanelli: Ken would have you think Davies his superior. Well, one writer about the tour employed adjectives which to my mind ring true. He called Davies 'elegant', Ken 'sublime'. Moreover, Terry McLean, the doyen of New Zealand rugby writers, raved about Ken ghosting 'like summer down through the New Zealand defence'.

He graduated from Cambridge in 1960 and from then on rugby could no longer have priority. He was soon married to his girlfriend of several years and would be a father twelve months later. He worked in a manufacturing firm in the English Midlands, and now had to juggle family responsibilities, work and rugby, as was of course normal for players in the amateur days. The demands were considerable, one reason why international careers were shorter then than they are now. He played for a couple of seasons for Leicester, though distance from home and work meant that he saw his new teammates only on match days. Training and practice were done on his own.

He captained Scotland in 1963, playing the last two matches in his schoolboy position of fly-half. That summer a change of employment took him to Aberdeen and this heralded the end of his international career. In those days, before the building of road bridges over the Tay and Forth, the journey to Edinburgh was slow and arduous. With a young family and sometimes work on Saturday morning, travel to Edinburgh to play for Heriot's FP would have been difficult, sometimes impossible, and also selfish. So he joined Aberdeenshire, an agreeable club with, however, what may politely be called a low-level fixture list. He probably lost some sharpness. At any rate the selectors were unimpressed. His place in the Scotland team went to Oxford University's Stewart Wilson, himself good enough to be a Lion in 1966, and though Ken was recalled for one match in 1965, his international career ended when he was only twenty-eight.

He continued to play club rugby for Aberdeenshire and for the North-Midlands in the Districts Championship for several years. The last time I saw him play was for the North-Midlands against the touring Australians in November 1968. It was a bitterly cold day with a stiff chilling wind coming off the North Sea, finger-nipping weather. He didn't put a foot wrong, gave an immaculate display. I have one vivid pictorial memory of the game. He fielded a kick on the right touchline about forty metres out. He was facing touch as he caught the ball, swivelled and unleashed a left-foot drop-kick. It soared high. From my position I thought it had flown just over the near-side post or just inside it. The referee judged it wide. I suppose a TMO might have judged differently, but this of course was long before the days of video evidence. No matter; it was a moment of the highest class.

Where does Ken rank among Scottish full-backs? It's a position in which, unlike many others, we have been richly blessed: Stewart Wilson, Andy Irvine, Bruce Hay, Peter Dods, Gavin Hastings, Chris Paterson, Stuart Hogg. It's a distinguished list. Some will remark that while several of his successors have been prolific try-scorers, he didn't score even one try in his twenty-seven international matches. To this I would reply first that he played in the most restrictive era of international rugby, when the laws favoured defence to such an extent that you might have thought they had been devised to make try-scoring difficult; only eleven tries were scored in the seven Calcutta Cup matches in which he played. Second, that he was a creator rather than scorer of tries. Comparisons of players from different times are probably pointless. So much in the game has changed. So I can say only that at his best he played beautiful rugby and I have never seen a more complete full-back than Ken Scotland. He played classical rugby with a romantic touch.

I suppose most who read this book will do so because of the rugby. But it has a wider interest too, especially when he recounts his work for the National Trust for Scotland. Perhaps he is not a natural autobiographer for he is not introspective, and is less interested in himself than in the world he has lived in. He is always generous in his treatment of others and he isn't interested in telling even mildly scandalous stories. He has offered a record of his outward life, an engaging record, which also offers a picture of middle-class Scotland and the changes it has experienced over the last seventy or eighty years. I think he is embarrassed by praise even when the praise has been fully earned. So I had better stop, and give way to his memories.

Allan Massie
September 2020

INTRODUCTION

When I left George Heriot's School, Edinburgh, in the summer of 1955, just a few weeks short of my nineteenth birthday, I had three ambitions in life. Sport of all kinds had always been my main interest and ever since my first visit to Murrayfield to watch Scotland play, and beat, the previously unbeaten New Zealand Army touring team, in January 1946, I had an all-consuming passion to play rugby for Scotland.

Being at an all-boys school, and with my sister Elsie eight years younger, I had very little to do with girls. Finding a partner to take to school dances had always been a problem until I struck gold with Doreen Marshall at Easter 1954. From surprisingly early in our relationship the only question was, when could we be married?

During my last year at school, Ian Reid, who was a contemporary, and who had been both captain and dux of the school, won an open scholarship to Trinity College, Cambridge. At that time, Heriot's had no connections with any Oxford or Cambridge colleges, but Ian's success opened a relationship between the senior admissions tutor at Trinity, J M K Vyvian, and our headmaster, William McLachlan Dewar.

During the rest of his time as headmaster, Dr Dewar developed this relationship and a succession of Heriot's boys went to Trinity. I was the first to benefit from Ian's scholarship and Dr Dewar's foresight and perseverance. Without my ever going to Cambridge or meeting anyone from Trinity, Dr Dewar managed to secure a place for me provided that I passed my current year's Scottish Leaving Certificate Exams. The sting in the tail was that it was mandatory to have passed a Latin exam and my only language qualification was French.

This possible change of direction came totally out of the blue. I was working to a specific timetable geared towards my chosen career as a chartered accountant. At that time training to become a CA was done through an apprenticeship in a professional office and I had never given a thought to going to university. Never in my wildest dreams had I ever imagined myself as an undergraduate at Cambridge.

Did I want to change track? What would my parents think and could they afford it? What would Doreen think and could our relationship and long-term plans survive the inevitable separations?

With encouragement from everyone involved I decided that the opportunity of going to Cambridge was too good to miss. In the course of the next few months I passed my year's exams and my father, through his legal connections, managed to unearth a very generous grant from the 'Sir Alexander Cross Trust' which allowed me to be virtually financially independent at Cambridge.

As I had still done no Latin up to this point it was decided that I would have to defer taking up my place at Trinity for a year. One year became two as I no longer had any reasonable grounds to avoid being called up for National Service.

Thus my third ambition was to pass a Latin exam. On the face of it a fairly modest ambition but it was to prove difficult and time consuming and, in the event, went right down to the wire.

ONE

THE GENES

It is only since I retired that I have taken more than a very superficial interest in my family background. As all the previous generations are now dead, there is no one left to ask the personal questions that are not covered in the statutory documents.

In my youth there were no mobile phones, iPads, computers, television or mass air travel, all of which the present generation takes for granted. I would like to give them some insight into how and where their ancestors lived and worked.

According to Black's *History of Scottish Surnames* the Scotland surname is said to derive from the village of Scotlandwell on the north-east shore of Loch Leven. By the beginning of the 17th century our branch of the family had moved a few miles west into the Dollar area of Clackmannanshire.

In 1662, two years after the restoration of Charles II to the British throne, a Scottish Parliament meeting in Edinburgh, passed an Act giving bishops a role in the Church of Scotland. Thomas and John Scotland, a father and son from Dollarbeg, were fined, along with 700-800 other lairds or landowners, for being against this Anglicisation of their church.

Dollarbeg by the end of that century had been split into Easter, our ancestors' area, and Wester. By the beginning of the 18th century Easter Dollarbeg had been divided again and our family, headed by John Scotland born 1713, was living and farming at Wellhall, a farm which still exists.

My great-great-great-grandfather, John Scotland, was born at Wellhall in 1736, exactly 200 years before me.

During the 18th century, there were great changes in agriculture. Fields were enlarged and enclosed and methods were intensified. This process produced winners and losers and by the beginning of the next century James Scotland (born 1775), my great-great-grandfather, had lost the land at Wellhall and was working as a master carter at Dollar South Mains.

William Scotland, my great-grandfather, born in 1830, was the seventh child of James Scotland and his wife Mary, nee Brand. In *Some Reminiscences of Dollar and Dollar Folk*, written in 1895 the Rev. John C Stewart described William as the son of the widow Mrs Scotland whose husband was killed in an accident at Gloomhill Quarry. 'William was a great boy for rabbits in his school days and many a time I helped to gather great bunches of dandelions for their food. William was one of nature's gentlemen.'

William and his younger sister Ann were both, in 1841, gratis scholars at the recently founded Dollar Institution (it became the more familiar Dollar Academy in 1918). This means they attended the school free and would be supplied with books and, if necessary, boots and clothing.

In 1858, William was working as a shoemaker in Alva when he married Ann Morrison. Ann died childless in 1875. A year later the forty-six-year-old widower remarried, in Edinburgh, twenty-year-old Margaret Bews from Stenness in Orkney, then working as a domestic servant in the Broughton district of Edinburgh. It remains a mystery how they ever met.

In 1878, my grandfather, James Scotland, was born in Alva. A year later William died and Margaret was left in strange surroundings to bring up her infant son. As far as I know Margaret thereafter had no contact with her Scotland in-laws, which makes the Bews and the Orkney connection a major part of my heritage.

In 1888, Margaret's father, James Bews, appealed to the Crofters Commission for a rent reduction. 'The area of my croft is six acres arable and outrun five acres. My rent is £3.00 and my arrears £4.10 shillings. I have reclaimed three acres and expended £2.00 on improvements.' The decision was a reduction in rent from £3.00 to £2.5 shillings.

Tracking the movements of Margaret and her son through the ten-yearly censuses shows that in 1881 James was staying with his grandparents in Orkney and that Margaret was working as a servant at her previous address in Edinburgh. In 1891 Margaret was working as a living-in nurse in Kirkcaldy (for the Nairn family of linoleum fame) and James a scholar at age thirteen was on his own at 165 Rose Street, Edinburgh. Ten years later Margaret was still nursing, at an address in Ferry Road, Edinburgh and James was shown as a tailor on his own in Wardie Crescent. Margaret had had a hard life and her last two and a half years were spent in the Royal Asylum at Morningside where she died of a cerebral haemorrhage in 1920 at the age of sixty-three.

In 1904 James married Elizabeth Scott, a girl from the south side of Glasgow. They lived in Edinburgh at Wardie Crescent, Comelybank Row and Murieston Terrace before settling down in Merchiston Grove where they brought up my father John William Bews (born 1905), Margaret Robina Burns (born 25 January 1907) and James Christie Elliott (born 1916). Elizabeth died of TB in 1924 at the age of forty-five and Auntie Peggy took on the role of running the household.

My grandfather was a constant presence in the first eight years of my life. Every Sunday, after attending his church in Gorgie Road, he would come in through our back door, hang up his coat, where he always had a sweetie for his grandchildren, and have his tea. To my eyes he was a distinguished-looking old man and, as would be expected from a tailor, always smartly dressed. His uncle, John Bews, was a tailor in St Stephen Street, Edinburgh as my grandfather was growing up and I assume that that is where he learned his trade.

As a small boy, I was taken to see him in his workshop at the same address in Rose Street where he had been recorded in a census about 50 years previously. I remember climbing a narrow stair to the room where he was working. The address was almost directly across from Ma Scott's pub and I was told many years later by my Uncle Jim that my grandfather had been a good customer.

My father, John – always known as Jack – attended Craiglockhart Primary School before moving on as a chorister to St. Mary's Cathedral Choir School. The cathedral played a major part in the rest of his life. As well as singing in the choir for at least fifty years he carried the cross at Matins for many, many years.

It was due to a recommendation from the cathedral that, at a meeting of the curators of the Advocates Library on 20 November 1919, a boy named John Scotland was appointed to work in the Law Room at Parliament House at a wage of ten shillings a week. This turned out to be his one and only place of work. By 1928 he had proved himself sufficiently to be appointed as an assistant advocate's clerk and by 1938 he was one of the four senior advocate's clerks. At the outbreak of war in 1939, the two youngest clerks were called up to serve in the armed forces and the other two, including my father, remained at Parliament House to help keep the law courts functioning.

His settled bachelor lifestyle, centred round the cathedral, Parliament House and supporting the Heart of Midlothian Football Club, changed when he joined Ravelston Tennis Club, sadly now disappeared under a block of flats. The tennis club would appear to have been a latter-day dating agency and there my father met and courted my mother Edith Forbes, who he married in September 1934.

Edith was descended from Alexander Forbes, my great-great-great-grandfather who was, circa 1800, doubling up as a crofter of a few acres and innkeeper at Bridge of Gairn, now on the outskirts of Ballater. There are family gravestones in the local cemetery dating from that time. This area to the north of Ballater was broken up into small farms/crofts and during the 19th century there were several intermarriages between the Forbeses, Lamonds, Rosses, and Patersons. Through the 19th century succeeding generations of Forbeses were shepherds or general farm labourers until, in the 1890s, my grandfather John Forbes (born 1873) found employment as a coachman, at Belnacroft, near Crathie, and then on the Grant estate at Rothiemurchus, near Aviemore before his work took him to Edinburgh.

My grandmother Elsie Grant was born in Rothes in 1867, one of three illegitimate children, by different fathers, of Jane Ann Watson. Elsie was brought up firstly by her Watson grandparents in Rothes and latterly by her extended Grant family in Grantown on Spey.

John Forbes and Elsie Grant were married in Grantown-on-Spey in 1895.

My mother, Edith, was the only surviving child of John and Elsie. An elder sister died in infancy.

By the time my mother was born in 1904 my grandfather was working as a barman and the family were living in Grindlay Street, Edinburgh. Two years later my grandfather died. As a one-parent family, life must have been extremely hard for them but my mother did so well at Tollcross Primary School that she won a George Heriot Bursary, awarded to fatherless children, which allowed her to continue her education at Boroughmuir Senior School. Her social life revolved round St Cuthbert's Church, not far from home, and, after she started work, with her colleagues in the Hope Street Post Office. The decision she made to join Ravelston Tennis Club, along with her friend Tibbie Phillips, led to the start of another branch in the Scotland family tree.

TWO

NURTURE

My parents were married on 1 September 1934 and their first home, in Warriston Avenue, was part of a recently completed development of approximately 100 four-apartment houses in the Goldenacre district of Edinburgh. The cost of the apartment was about £400, which they had saved before they married.

I was born at 28 Warriston Avenue, Edinburgh on 29 August 1936, the first child of Jack and Edith (nee Forbes) Scotland.

My first memory is being sent to tell the news of my brother Ronnie's birth in July 1938 to my (honorary) Auntie Mary who lived a few houses down the Avenue.

In 1941, I started at George Heriot's School along with David Brown, David Smith, Derek McCracken and Eddie McKeating who were all Warriston neighbours. Derek and Eddie have remained lifelong friends and no story of my schooldays would be complete without Eddie in particular taking centre stage. Every morning we caught a tram at the end of Warriston Gardens which took us to school, directly opposite the Royal Infirmary in Lauriston Place. Heriot's was then a boys-only school of about 1,500 pupils from age five to eighteen. The Warriston development which consisted predominantly of first-time buyers was by the early 1940s awash with school age children. The fathers went out to work in offices and shops and the mums stayed at home. In what I have always imagined was the Scottish tradition, parents wanted to give their children the best education that they could afford and we nearly all went to fee-paying schools. The boys went to the Academy, Heriot's, Melville, Stewart's or Watson's and the girls to Gillespies, Queen Street or Watson's.

Quite by chance, I made the same journey on the upper deck of a bus over seventy years later and it was quite amazing how little had changed. Instead of a twenty-three or twenty-seven tram it was now the same choice of buses taking the identical route. Starting at my spiritual home of the playing fields at Goldenacre the journey passed the Royal Botanic Gardens, crossed over the Water of Leith at Canonmills, passed through the New Town with historic names like Pitt Street, Dundas Street and Cumberland Street up hill to George Street, down Hanover Street facing the Royal Scottish Academy, across Princes Street with views of Calton Hill and the Scott monument to the left, up the Mound past the National Gallery on the left with the unique architecture of Ramsey Gardens and the backdrop of the Castle on the right, on past the head office of the Bank of Scotland up and over the Royal Mile with a glimpse of St Giles Cathedral and the law courts, then on opposite sides of George IV Bridge the National Library and the Edinburgh Public Library, on past Greyfriar's Bobby with the historic churchyard behind and finally turning into Lauriston Place with (in 1941) the Royal Infirmary on the left and my destination for the next fourteen years on the right, George Heriot's School. Surely some of the finer things in life must have rubbed off on that daily journey.

George Heriot was a successful goldsmith in Edinburgh with two of his best clients being King James VI and his Danish consort Queen Anna. With the Union of the Crowns in 1603 George Heriot followed the Royal Household to London where his business continued to flourish. When he died in 1624, he left the bulk of his fortune to found, in Edinburgh, a 'School' in imitation of Christ's Hospital which had been founded in London in 1552 and, by the time of Heriot, was established as an orphanage as well as a school for poor children.

The foundation stone for the school was laid on an eight-and-a-half-acre site, overlooked by the castle, in 1628. It took until 1650 for the building to be more or less complete and the first occupants were wounded soldiers from Cromwell's army during his siege of the castle.

Heriot's bequest to be used for the education of 'faitherless bairns' is still in existence today with a proportion of the pupils paying no fees.

After school, as there was no through-road in our part of Warriston, we were able to play all sorts of games in the street. Football was probably the most popular with the boys, although not for the neighbours who took their gardens seriously, but we also played levoy, peevers and kick-the-can to name a few that I can remember. The streets were almost devoid of traffic as virtually no family owned a car. We also played in three large areas of waste ground, known by us as the backies, fronties, now housing estates, and cockies, now Goldenacre Bowling Club, but what was to become the focus for me was the adjacent playing fields of George Heriot's School at Goldenacre.

The Second World War was an ever-present background to my life from age three to nine. However, I was lucky that it had little direct effect. Very few of the fathers in the street went away to the war. Dad was in the Home Guard and spent many evenings, and occasionally the whole night, fire watching from their base in the stand at Goldenacre. I do remember, however, overhearing hushed conversations about the son of our next-door neighbours who was in the 8th Army in North Africa, and at the great sense of relief when he eventually came home on leave.

When I started school, everyone had to carry a gasmask but that precaution was relaxed fairly quickly. There was an air-raid shelter built in a neighbour's garden and in the event of the air-raid siren going all our immediate neighbours congregated in it until the all-clear siren sounded. Fortunately, I can only remember spending a handful of nights in the shelter. Edinburgh largely escaped the bombing but German aircraft regularly passed over the city on their way to bomb the shipyards on the Clyde. The sound made by a siren can still sent a shiver up my spine.

Other obvious signs that the country was at war were the removal of all the iron railings and gates from the district and the ploughing of about a quarter of the playing fields at Goldenacre and four holes at my father's golf club at Barnton.

During the war there were also restrictions on travel. The first holiday I remember was in 1942 to a farm in Drem. I had a broken arm in plaster at the time and apart from letting the pigs out of their sty I don't remember any other excitement. Also during the war we went for an annual fortnight's holiday to Lundin Links where we met the Lightbody family from Leven. The Lightbodys became good friends and we subsequently shared holidays with them in Cullen, Carnoustie, Prestwick and Llandudno.

Our family was completed when sister Elsie was born at Warriston Avenue in November 1944. It says much for my powers of observation and for the lack of openness in these matters at that time that the birth came to me as a complete surprise.

In the summer of 1945 – ostensibly to give Mum a rest – Dad took Ronnie and me away for a holiday to St Fillans. The highlight of this visit was taking part in the celebrations to mark VJ (Victory in Japan) Day on the banks of Loch Earn, which finally signalled the end of the Second World War.

By that time my life had developed a fairly distinct weekly pattern. On week days I went to school, and as soon as I got home I changed into sports kit and headed, summer and winter, for the playing fields at Goldenacre. On Friday evenings I went to the 4th Leith Cubs. On Saturdays there were rugby or cricket matches to watch. On Sundays, until my voice broke, I sang in the choir at St. James Episcopal Church at Goldenacre. Four services on the first Sunday of the month, otherwise only two. About this age I discovered I was definitely a Saturday person as that was the only day I happily got out of bed.

Although the war was now over, rationing of food and clothing was still in operation and austerity was the watchword throughout the country. Needless to say, I find the modern trend towards conspicuous consumption tasteless in the extreme. My main memory of early Christmases was putting together my presents of book-tokens and money and heading uptown to buy books. £1 then was sufficient to buy eight paperback Biggles or The Saint or my favourite Teddy Lester School Story books.

By the end of 1945 I must have watched every rugby and cricket match played at Goldenacre for the previous three or four years and by hanging around and looking desperate to join in I had had a fair amount of experience playing both cricket and rugby with older boys.

Also, I had been lucky to be taken to watch Services representative games played at the old international ground at Inverleith. For me, however, the life-dominating event was being taken to Murrayfield for the first time on 19 January 1946 to watch Scotland play the unbeaten New Zealand Army touring team. The big crowd, the atmosphere in general and the fact that Scotland had won a famous victory all had a big effect on me.

Up to that point my big ambition had been to play for the school on the stand pitch at Goldenacre. From that day at Murrayfield, the one continuing, all-consuming passion and ambition in my life, day and night, was to one day play rugby for Scotland.

My first step towards this goal and my first official game of school sport was a practice game with thirty ten-year-olds running about chasing the ball like headless chickens. I attempted to drop a goal and although I can't remember whether it was successful or not it was sufficient evidence for me to be chosen immediately to play stand-off for the 1st Juniors.

Although rugby was my number one winter sport, I also enjoyed playing football. Up to the age of fourteen, by getting to school early and playing during my lunch break, I would usually manage to fit in half an hour's worth of 'tanner ba'' football. I think playing football helped me develop, particularly, a sense of balance and two-footedness which would have been harder to acquire playing rugby only.

Of all the football I played, I can only remember four games with goalposts and nets. At Cambridge I played once for Trinity in a Cuppers match and when I lived in Aberdeen I played once for the concrete factory team and twice to raise money for the 1970 Commonwealth Games to be held at Meadowbank in Edinburgh. The two games were for a team of rugby players against a team of ex-Aberdeen footballers. The first was at Linksfield in Aberdeen and the second in Elgin. That effort was well worthwhile as I was an excited spectator at Meadowbank the day Scots Ian Stewart and Ian McCafferty beat the favourite Kip Keino in the 5,000 metres.

The summer term was devoted mainly to cricket but holidays allowed time to fit in a bit of golf and tennis.

When I moved up to the senior school at age twelve in 1948, I had had two years playing at stand-off for the 1st Juniors at rugby and as a batsman/wicketkeeper at cricket.

*

My move into the senior school coincided with changes for myself and more importantly for the school. By that time, I had acquired a basic understanding of the three Rs, then the staple minimum, of reading writing and arithmetic. There was no concern then regarding the political correctness of streaming. In Senior 1a the brightest did Latin, 1b did German, 1c and 1d did French and 1e and 1f did Spanish. To our basic English and maths we all added history and geography and physics, chemistry and natural sciences. I found my level doing French in 1d.

Even to a twelve-year-old it was evident that the school was being run from the staff room rather than the headmaster's office. This changed with the appointment of William McL Dewar as headmaster quickly followed by Donald Hastie as games master. They both came from Greenock Academy. Dr Dewar's appointment broke the tradition of promotion from within and prior to Mr Hastie's arrival, as a 'professional games master' all school sport had been organised on a voluntary basis by members of the teaching staff. Both were given an extremely hard time by the existing staff but I think that most pupils, if they thought about it at all, quite quickly concluded that they were exactly what was needed to drive the school forward. They both subsequently became major influences for good in my life.

Also important to me in 1948 was that Ireland won the Triple Crown with stand-off J W (Jackie) Kyle being their acknowledged playmaker. From then on, I tried to model my game in his image. Just how I decided what his game was is a bit of a mystery to me now because at most I only saw him play in the flesh two or three times and of course there was then neither television or the video replay on which to analyse his every move. In my mind, I saw him mainly as a tactically kicking stand-off who, when he got into an attacking position, moved the ball quickly to his centres. He was very sparing in attempts to make a break – but when he did, it was usually decisive and at a critical stage of the game. The other important part of his game was cover tackling but with the understanding that it was his wing forwards' job to do all the head-on defensive chores.

My other big sporting hero was Godfrey Evans, the Kent and England wicketkeeper. He was one of the main attractions at the Festival of Sport held at the Waverley Market in Edinburgh in the early 1950s. He gave me a few tips and I still have a signed copy of his book *Behind the Stumps*, which became a treasured possession.

The first three years of senior school were important academically, if only to prove that I had no aptitude for science subjects. Sport was still very much the dominant factor in my life and my joined-at-the-hip relationship with Eddie McKeating was forged. Eddie was born three days after me, and about 200 yards away, and we started school in the same class on the same day. The school was divided into four houses for all sorts of different competitions. Castle, Greyfriars and Lauriston were obvious dominant features surrounding the school, but Eddie and I were assigned to Raeburn, named after the famous portrait painter who had been educated at Heriot's.

What threw us together and made us slightly different was that until our voices broke we sang in the local Episcopal church choir while all our other friends went to St Serfs, the Church of Scotland parish church.

In my late teens, my life revolved around the school. After an early association with the 4th Leith Cubs and Scouts, linked with St Serfs Church, I changed my allegiance to the Scottish Schoolboys Club (SSC), another outlet for 'muscular Christianity'.

A typical week at that time began with family attendance at the cathedral on Sunday morning, followed, in the early years, by an evening game of tennis at Westhall and, later, by a game of cricket for the Grange. In winter afternoons, there were SSC discussion groups to attend. My tennis career peaked at the age of fourteen when I reached the semi-final of the East of Scotland Boys Doubles. To put this achievement into perspective I was beaten 6–0, 6–0, in the singles by my partner, the late irrepressible Ronnie Bateman.

Monday was school. Tuesday was school followed by either rugby or cricket practice. In the summer, we had a cricket match after school on a Wednesday. Thursday was identical to Tuesday. On Friday immediately after school I had a parade with the RAF section of the cadet force and, after a quick change out of uniform at home, it was back to school for a meeting of the Literary and Dramatic Society. I neither acted nor took part in debates but because of my known ambition to become an accountant I was elected treasurer of the 'Lit'.

Saturday morning was playing rugby or cricket followed by spectating in the afternoon. In the evening it could be back to school for an SSC club night or perhaps to another school for a meeting of the Edinburgh Schools Citizenship Association, which was always popular as that involved the possibility of speaking to a girl. In the early years, it could be a night out at the pictures and later to dances, often at Craiglockhart Tennis Club, but also at a variety of other dance halls.

Holidays were also dominated by school activities. At Easter there was always an SSC camp and once we had a Corps camp in the south of England which meant, for most of us, the excitement of travelling through London for the first time. In the summers we again had a Corps camp in the south of England and also a longer version of an SSC Camp.

The SSC had a positive influence on my life and it also gave me the opportunity to meet boys from other schools other than on the sports fields. I still meet an old Royal High School friend from those days, Jimmy Jarvis, for an occasional weekend beer when we mourn the death of yet another contemporary, commiserate about each other's latest aches and pains and generally put the world to rights.

School cricket was very popular in the 1950s and in a short season we played on average fifteen matches against other schools and local clubs. The school employed as cricket coach/groundsman a former Glamorgan player, Arthur Creber, who along with school teacher LL (Lindsay) Mitchell provided great encouragement and enthusiasm, particularly to the younger players. They realised that in most school teams five or six of the senior players did most of both the batting and bowling. Their answer was to feed two or three young boys into the side to give them experience to develop into the next generation of senior players. Eddie McKeating and I both benefited from this policy and had six seasons in the 1st XI. By the time we became the senior players, two further youngsters thrived on this policy. George Goddard and Hamish More joined the 1955 XI (which was captained by Eddie) and went on to play cricket for Scotland.

As well as having an unbeaten season, the team went on to accumulate the following honours: a Scottish cricket captain with 124 caps and two MCC 'A' overseas tours, British Schools 100-yards champion, a Scottish rugby captain with thirty-three Scotland caps and five British and Irish Lions caps and captain of Cambridge University rugby, and seven players who played in the Melrose Sevens, winning seven gold and six silver medals.

THREE

MY FIRST INTERNATIONAL – OF SORTS

It shouldn't come as a surprise that I was in no hurry to leave school. Having just turned eighteen and passed sufficient Highers to get into the sixth year, I returned for a final session, as school captain. At that time, I was aiming for a career as a chartered accountant and a personal timetable was constructed with that in mind. I already had certain exemptions from the Institute of Chartered Accountants and a pass in the finance and statistics paper would allow me to start an apprenticeship in a professional office with all their first intermediate exams behind me. I would also spend time at classes to upgrade my maths pass from lower to higher.

All was set fair for a final season of school rugby with Eddie McKeating as captain and myself as his deputy. We had a pretty good understanding on the pitch and in a way our strengths were complementary, he ran and tackled and I passed and kicked.

Up until the Christmas holidays, as a XV we had scored quite freely and had ambitions to create a points-scoring record. Also, the school record for the number of tries in a season, twenty-four, just happened to be held by our current master in charge of rugby, George Blamire, and Eddie was closing in fast on that figure.

Our only loss, and probably the best game we played, was against Merchiston Castle. Although it was a low-scoring game, 3–9, it was played at pace and full of physicality. Two of the Merchiston side, Calum Bannerman and Cameron Boyle, were to become close friends of mine, but more of that later.

The following appeared in the *Merchiston School Magazine* summing up their season: 'Then came Heriot's, certainly the most attractive side of the season with splendid backs led by the stand-off, Scotland, a brilliant player of exceptional promise. For ten minutes they were all over us and scored a lovely try with the ease and class of internationals demonstrating how it should be done. But thereafter the defence held, and gradually our forwards asserted themselves and in the second half so dominated the game that we were able to inflict on our opponents their only defeat of the season. The whole side played very, very well, but the abiding memory of the match will be the genius of Scotland, who was as good in adversity in the later stages as he had been in those sparkling opening minutes.'

On Monday 27 December, the annual schools intercity match between Edinburgh and Glasgow was played at Old Anniesland in Glasgow with six Heriot's boys, including Eddie and I (I was named as captain), in the Edinburgh side which won 13–0 in very windy conditions.

In the *Daily Express*, Jock Wemyss wrote: 'Quite outstanding was Edinburgh's skipper and stand-off, Kenneth Scotland. The Heriot's captain showed real class in everything he did and his judgement of whether to run to pass or to kick made him look like an experienced senior.'

After the game we were joined by the rest of our Heriot's school team and we left from the Broomielaw on the overnight ferry to Belfast on our way to Dublin.

On Wednesday 29, we played our return fixture against Belvedere College at Jones' Road, Dublin, winning narrowly 16–9.

For Eddie and I it was straight on to the steamer for Holyhead and the overnight sleeper to London where we were met and looked after by Mr. Gibbs, president of the London Heriot's Club. At lunchtime on Friday 31 December, he dropped us off at a restaurant in Richmond where we met the rest of the London Scottish Schools XV.

There was no official age grade representative rugby at that time but this holiday fixture was, for all intents and purposes, an age-grade international. A 'Scotland' and an 'England' team were selected by London Scottish and Richmond respectively and the match was played at the Richmond Athletic Ground where they were joint-tenants.

The Scottish team were not all complete strangers to us as we had had a practice session with the four Fettesians in the team, at Fettes, which was within walking distance of our homes in Edinburgh. As this included the half-backs Gordon Waddell and David Horne, our back division started with a bit of an advantage. Most of the others we were meeting for the first time.

In truth the England XV were probably complete strangers to each other and the familiarity of our combinations probably made a crucial difference. Our team came together very well and we recorded a very convincing 29–3 victory.

Michael Melford in the *Daily Telegraph* wrote: 'It is no doubt easier to locate the best players in the more parochial world of Scottish school football and their side certainly had the advantage of combination. The Fettes halves, Waddell, a son of H Waddell, fifteen times capped for Scotland, and Horne worked beautifully together and the Heriot's right-wing pair, Scotland and McKeating, were a joy to watch. Scotland, wonderfully quick into his stride, had a hand in all five tries. He rounded off a spectacular exhibition of handling by catching full toss a long cross-kick from Gibbons on the other touch-line and sending McKeating in for the last of his three tries.'

This was the first of many games that I played and enjoyed with Gordon Waddell. Son of Herbert, the stand-off in Scotland's 1925 Grand Slam-winning team, Gordon was nurtured in all the tactical possibilities of playing in that position. I came to know Gordon's game almost as well as my own. On our side Brian Neill went on to captain Scotland, and Tony Peart, the opposition No. 8, went on to play for England.

Three years later, when I played for Cambridge University LX Club against Oxford University Greyhounds, the respective captains were both from that London Scottish Schools XV back row. Hector Kirsop, ex-Fettes, for the Greyhounds, and Francis Walker, ex-Edinburgh Academy, for the LX Club.

The following year, playing with Gordon for Cambridge University against Oxford University, we were joined by David Bird and Pat Mills who had been in the opposition at Richmond.

After tea in the clubhouse at Richmond, which was later to become one of my favourite rugby haunts, Eddie and I made our way to King's Cross to catch an overnight train back to Edinburgh. It wasn't the most comfortable of trips north, but we did have time to buy a half bottle of port and a couple of screwtops to help us bring in the New Year in traditional fashion.

When next I met Norman Mair (later a distinguished rugby and golf correspondent for *The Scotsman*) he suggested that the result at Richmond was the sort of habit that Scots should get into. Sadly, that turned out to be the only time I played on a winning side against England.

The second half of the rugby season was an anti-climax. Most games were cancelled because of frozen pitches and our target of record points-scored never even came close, although Eddie did end up with twenty-four tries to equal that record. We finished the season with a bit of a flourish by winning sevens tournaments at Paisley Grammar School, Hillhead High School, Murrayfield and our own school's inaugural tournament at Goldenacre.

A highlight at the end of the season was a bus trip to Twickenham organised by our rugby master, George Blamire. Scotland had emerged from a run of seventeen successive defeats and were travelling to London looking for an elusive Triple Crown. George and one other teacher took charge of a bus load of seventeen- and eighteen-year-olds. We had a very good view of the game. We clearly saw Tom Elliot's winning try, but unfortunately the referee didn't, which meant that another opportunity to record a rare win at Twickenham – and an even rarer Triple Crown – had gone begging. After the game, the bus dropped us all off in Piccadilly Circus with instructions to be back at midnight for the return journey. The two teachers disappeared and we were left to our own devices. Not the level of supervision that teachers would get away with nowadays.

It was around this time in early 1955 that what had seemed to be my clear career path was quite suddenly turned on its head. Totally unexpectedly, the chance of going to Cambridge University became a possibility. It took several hectic weeks of sorting out a variety of problems, but with help from the school and with support from Doreen and my family I was encouraged to accept the opportunity.

With this decision made I was able to enjoy my last term at school. To two cricket matches a week for the school I usually managed to add a senior Sunday game for the Grange cricket club. The two highest scores of my batting career came just after leaving school when one weekend I scored 136 for the Grange against Scottish Command, followed two days later by 138 for the Heriot's FP cricket club against The Runagates, a team on tour from the Newcastle area.

Under the influence of Donald Hastie, the school ran a very

successful athletics club with regular contests against other schools. I competed reasonably successfully in the half-mile but never quite managed to get my time down to two minutes.

A win in the half-mile and high jump and second place in the quarter-mile, behind a now golfing friend Bob Hay, and long jump enabled me to be runner-up in the games championship to Eddie McKeating.

In what was a distinctly non-vintage year, I managed to become school tennis champion. As it happened, tennis was the first sport I stopped playing and I rarely held a racquet after leaving school.

During a family holiday in St Andrews, in August, I received my call-up papers for National Service. In the aftermath of the Second World War all healthy males, who were not conscientious objectors, were at the age of eighteen conscripted into one of the armed forces. Call-up could be deferred while still in full time education and was eventually phased out in the early 1960s.

Doreen was also on holiday with her family and we 'celebrated', with friends Brendan Lynch and Sandy Gillies, amongst others, in the Cross Keys Hotel. While unknowingly being plied with Carlsberg Specials I was introduced to the intricacies of 'Cardinal Puff'. It was a memorable send-off.

FOUR

KHAKI RUGBY

By the time I left school in July 1955, I had become a big fish in a small pool and I now had three ambitions in life. To playing rugby for Scotland, I had added getting into Cambridge and marrying my girlfriend, Doreen Marshall.

Realistically, the older I got the more unlikely my number-one project became. Tommy Hall of Dollar Academy, Colin McCulloch of Melville College and Gordon Waddell of Fettes had all been selected ahead of me for Edinburgh or London Scottish teams and two future Scotland stand-offs, Iain Laughland at Merchiston and Gregor Sharp at Stewart's, were also playing school rugby in Edinburgh at that time.

Two months after leaving school, on Thursday 1 September 1955, I reported for two years' National Service in the Royal Signals at Catterick Camp, near Darlington, Yorkshire. Now Signalman Scotland, 23173022, I had become a very small fish indeed in a very large pool. The first day was long, tiring, demeaning and traumatic and when eventually the lights went out the prospect of another 730 similar days seemed unendurable. There were a few in that intake who had never previously been away from home and they really suffered. It was also an eye-opener to realise that others needed help to write the obligatory letter home, which arrived in a parcel with all our civilian clothes, to say that we had arrived safely.

Having been a Flight Sergeant in the air force cadets at school, I was expected to opt to do my national service in the RAF but I had heard, from Ian Thomson and David Dakers, both Heriot's FP rugby players and cricketers, that the best place to go to get plenty of opportunities to play sport was the Signals. That first day at Catterick made me doubt my sanity.

Nearly sixty years later I could still manage to feel sorry for myself remembering that first day in the army until I heard my neighbour George Reid's story. During the war, at the age of eighteen, he was called up and opted to join the navy. On the way to his first posting at Skegness, the convoy was strafed by German planes and some of his colleagues were killed before they had even been issued with their uniforms. So much for my self-pity.

Although my civvies had all been packed off home I was allowed to hold on to my rugby boots, which did seem a good sign. In the same intake was Alan Smith who, amongst other achievements, toured Australia with the MCC and became MCC Secretary. Hoping for perhaps a month's cricket, he arrived with the full kit only to have it make a quick return journey along with his clothes.

After a few days of being harried from pillar to post and being introduced to genuine military square-bashing under the sadistic eye and voice of a 7th Training Regiment drill sergeant, I was relieved to get an order to appear at the sports field that evening for a sevens practice.

So it came about that on Saturday 10 September 1955, I made my senior rugby debut at the Kelso Sevens in the colours of Royal Signals, Catterick. The Royal Signals, I discovered, had won the tournament the previous year so we were defending the trophy. A loss to Kelso in the first round put paid to any storybook start to my career, but it did mean that perhaps my choice of service would be justified. It also meant a quicker than expected reunion with Doreen, but the scratchy khaki uniform wasn't much of a turn-on for either of us.

Although the trip to Kelso was unsuccessful, it did introduce me to the rugby that was available at Catterick. Royal Signals, Catterick, was a properly organised rugby club with a regular weekly Saturday fixture list against most of the top clubs in Yorkshire. They also had a decent Clubhouse, previously a sergeants' mess, and a good home pitch at Scotton, close to the barracks where I was doing my basic training.

Although there were a few regular soldiers in the team, the bulk of the players were only there for a maximum of two seasons, so the strength of the team could fluctuate quite widely. I was lucky that while the standard overall was good they were looking for a new recruit at stand-off, so I was immediately introduced to regular senior rugby.

After four weeks of basic training designed to make life as uncomfortable as possible and to instil an automatic and unquestioning response to any order no matter how unreasonable, I was ready for my first posting. Such time as I had for contemplation during these weeks largely confirmed what I already knew: by accident of birth, I had had a privileged childhood in a secure and loving family environment along with an all-round education at a school where the staff really cared about their pupils. Now I was on my own, I would hesitate to say that I became selfish but like all my fellow recruits I had to become totally self-reliant. There was no one there looking out for me.

My first posting was a short march through the camp to the Officers Training Wing (OTW). Having been selected as potential officer material, our basic training continued but at a more measured pace. We were introduced to the rifle range and taught how to use a bayonet. We completed obstacle courses and crawled through mud. At night we took turns to be on guard duty armed with pickaxe handles as the IRA had been known to attempt robberies of armouries at that time. We also had some leisure time to relax and spend our money in the NAAFI after a day's training.

I should have mentioned that I now had the novelty of being paid. The going rate was 7 shillings (35p) per day, less deductions for food and board, which ended up at 19 shillings and 7 pence per week (just under £1). For this princely sum we queued up weekly to be paid in cash. To put these figures into some context, a pie and a pint in the NAFFI cost 7.5p.

After four weeks at OTW, I went to Barton Stacey in Gloucestershire to attend a War Office Selection Board. It never even crossed my mind that I might fail, but fail I did.

All the purely physical tests went well but the main interview did not and, in particular, my reasons for joining the army rather than pursue my previous involvement with the RAF failed to convince. My chosen ten-minute talk on the origins of the Trade Union Movement may also not have been considered a suitable topic for the Officers' Mess. So it was back to Catterick with my tail firmly between my legs.

In purely rugby terms, failing my WOSB turned out to be helpful. From OTW I was posted, another short march through the camp, to train as a radio mechanic at 1 Training Regiment, Royal Signals. 1TR was the hotbed of all sports at Catterick and I was destined to spend the rest of my two years there, although I never quite made it as a radio mechanic.

My army career may have stalled but after only two months at Catterick I had played twelve games of rugby, at varying levels. Added to seven games for Royal Signals, Catterick, were two regimental games for OTW and three for Northern Command where the standard was definitely much higher. Two of the Command games were against full Northumberland and Yorkshire XVs at a time when county rugby was taken very seriously in England and was seen by their players as a stepping stone to international selection.

In November, I played three more Signals games before I was surprised to be picked at stand-off for the Whites in the first of three Scotland international trials to be held at Murrayfield. I survived to play in the second trial, where I was joined by my old school friend, Eddie McKeating, but I did not make the cut for the final trial. I think I was very fortunate to be starting my senior rugby well away from the critical eye of the Scottish press and rugby public. I got the opportunity to find my own level without weekly scrutiny of my performances.

On the day of the final trial, I played for Heriot's 2nd XV against Haddington and I was given plenty of advice from the senior players, especially Bill McMillan, who had had a particularly successful career as a sevens player, as to what I could and could not get away with in senior rugby. Nothing like being back home amongst friends to be brought down to earth.

Taking stock at the end of 1955, how were my ambitions shaping up? I have written mostly about rugby and I was definitely ahead of my expectations. I had really landed on my feet in Catterick and I doubt if I could have received a better all-round grounding anywhere else.

In my four months away, a mixture of leave and forty-eight- and thirty-six-hour passes, and the Scottish Rugby Union (SRU) paying my rail fare, allowed me to spend seventeen days at home and keep my romance with Doreen ticking over.

Not doing so well, however, was my pursuit of a Latin qualification. I had been given access to an Education Corps sergeant who was available to help but, so far, I hadn't found much time, or inclination, to work with him. On one visit to the Education Department I did, however, meet a friendly Aberdonian by the name of Eric Auld who became a very successful artist. We now have one of his Highland landscapes hanging in our living room.

Ex-national servicemen love to have a story of a skive. Having arrived at 1TR I had a week or two to fill in waiting for the next radio mechanics course to begin. Every morning, after breakfast, I attended the 'Fatigues Parade' in front of the Company Sergeant Major, and every morning I was assigned general duties at the rugby club.

The duties were actually non-existent and I became familiar with programmes on the wireless like *Workers Playtime* and Sandy MacPherson on the cinema organ. There was also plenty of opportunity to kick a ball about.

Just playing in the Scottish trials brought my name and Eddie McKeating's to the attention of the Services selectors and 1955 ended on a high with our selection to join a Combined Services short tour to the south of France. Exactly one year on from bringing in the New Year on an overnight train from London to Edinburgh with our screw-tops and half bottle of port, Eddie and I were supping champagne in a night club in Toulouse. Not too much, of course, because I was playing the next day, in the centre, against Mazamet, the home club of the massive Lucien Mias who, in 1959, captained the first French XV to win the Five Nations outright.

In early 1956, I played at stand off for the Army against Oxford University, Gloucester and Harlequins. These games represented a significant increase in speed and overall standard and I was lucky to be playing with a very experienced scrum-half in Dennis Shuttleworth. I was even luckier in that his regular regimental and Army stand-off Mike Hardy was unavailable that season. They had played together for England in the 1951

Calcutta Cup win over Scotland and were a particularly well-known partnership in English rugby at that time. Dennis undoubtedly helped me find my feet at that level.

These games were warm-ups for the real thing – the Inter Services Series to be played at Twickenham. My first big game was against the Navy and my opposite number was Norman Davidson, a former double Scottish internationalist. Norman was born and educated in Hawick, but when he got a cricket cap in 1951 and seven rugby caps from 1952–1954, he was a medical student and playing for Edinburgh University. In the ten years that I watched Scotland play at Murrayfield as a schoolboy, nine different stand-offs were selected – so, although I had watched Norman play and heard of him through cricket connections, I had no real impression of his style of play. Also having his first game at that level at scrum-half for the Navy was Tremayne Rodd. Tremayne went on to play fourteen times for Scotland and our paths were to cross at regular intervals, and he was in the team when I played my last international in Paris in 1965.

This game was watched by Scottish selector A H Brown, an ex-Scotland stand-off and Heriot's FP. My father happened to meet him during the week after the game and asked him if he had any advice to pass on. 'Tell Kenneth to get hold of a decent pair of shorts because the ones he was wearing were much too long and baggy and made him look ponderous.'

Not exactly what I wanted to hear, but thereafter I always made a point of being first into the team kitbag to sort out a pair of shorts.

What he was politely saying was that I looked off the pace. In fact, it was a fairly static forward battle in a drizzle which we won by two tries to one penalty. *The Times* rugby correspondent put it this way: 'Scotland, who is still in his teens, is worthy on Saturdays' form of the attention of the Scottish selectors, looking to the future, but he was fortunate to have as his partner the brave and experienced Shuttleworth capable of standing up to the Navy pack.'

It was straight back to Catterick for a regimental game on the Tuesday then on to Leicester to play for the Army against the Territorial Army on the Thursday. Meanwhile, the Scotland season had not gone well and, at the instigation of the Scottish selectors, I played my first game for Heriot's FP in Glasgow on the Saturday against the High School FPs. The stand-off position for the England game at Murrayfield on the following Saturday was very much up for grabs. My opposite number in the High School team was Donald Cameron, younger brother of Angus Cameron who had toured with the Lions in South Africa in 1955 and playing in the centre for them was Jimmy Docherty, a current Scotland player. In the event I had a poor game, making one or two glaringly obvious basic mistakes, and put myself out of contention. As Dennis Shuttleworth, who by this time had become a mentor to me, put it the next time we played together, 'the selectors did you a favour because you're not ready for that level.'

There were still two Army games, against the RAF and the French Army, to be played at Twickenham, so my season, and learning curve, was far from over. The contrast between my first year out of school and that of a current aspiring young Scottish stand-off could hardly be more different. I played forty-two games, and four sevens tournaments, varying from pretty low standard regimental games to the very competitive Inter Services Series.

In the first four months of 1956, as well as five home games in Catterick, I played in the south of France, Pembroke Dock in west Wales, Oxford, Gloucester, London four times, Nottingham, Leicester and Glasgow twice, Bath, Coventry, Edinburgh, Middlesborough, Hawick, Bradford and Huddersfield. During that time, 1TR Royal Signals won the Northern Command

Cup, Royal Signals Catterick won the Huddersfield Sevens (which Heriot's FP 3rd Seven had won three times in the early 1950s) and at Goldenacre Heriot's FP won the under-20 sevens tournament.

So after eight months in the army, my rugby ambition had progressed way beyond anything I could possibly have imagined, my romance was ticking over on very short rations but my Latin studying had more or less come to a full stop under the pressure of all the travelling.

Also not faring well was the Signals' effort to train me as a radio mechanic. It was an eight-week course with an exam after four weeks to qualify to continue. I failed the four-week exam several times, which was no surprise as I was seldom in Catterick for more than a few days at a time and I had no natural aptitude for anything practical or scientific. With no chance of me ever qualifying to stay in the regiment as a radio mechanic, I was promoted to Lance Corporal and given the post of Intake NCO. This involved, on a four-weekly cycle, marching a group of new recruits from their basic training to their first posting and making sure that they all found a billet.

The transition from rugby to cricket was more or less seamless and as it turned out the summer of 1956 was the peak of my cricket career. Regimental cricket was played to a good standard and as a wicket-keeper I particularly enjoyed the enthusiasm and quality of the fielding. As well as the Regiment, I also played for Catterick Services, the Royal Corps of Signals and Northern Command. The Inter-Corps games were played over two days and involved young professional cricketers doing their National Service, so the standard was high. The opposition included future Test cricketers such as John Edrich and Phil Sharpe and the previously mentioned Alan Smith and David Green, a future Cambridge captain, played for the Signals. Alan Smith, amongst other cricketing honours, went on the 1962 MCC tour of Australia as second wicket-keeper to John T Murray of Middlesex. Putting as positive a spin as possible on my ability, more often than not when we played together, I kept wicket.

I finished my first year in the Army playing for Northern Command against a Yorkshire 2nd XI featuring, as an opening batsman, a certain H D Bird who as Dickie Bird became a renowned Test umpire.

The 1956/57 rugby season started with a repeat, and equally unsuccessful, visit to the Kelso Sevens. During the months of September to November, I played regular Saturday club games for Royal Signals Catterick and midweek, Regimental fixtures and Northern Command representative matches.

It came as a slight disappointment to me that when the teams for the first Scottish trial were announced in early December I was not included. However, a few days before the trial I received an invitation by post to attend as a reserve full-back with the full-back heavily underlined. This was a surprise as my experience as a full-back was limited to only four or five games as a schoolboy five years previously.

On the Friday evening, my father met me when I arrived at the Waverley Station in Edinburgh with the news that Micky Grant had called off and that I was now playing full-back for the Whites in the trial at Hawick the following day. Robin Chisholm, the current holder of the position, was playing full-back for the Blues who also included my old school friend Eddie McKeating.

Trials always tend to have an unreal feeling and, with both teams travelling together on the train to Hawick, this feeling was particularly enhanced. The Blues were the nucleus of the previous season's Scotland XV and the Whites were a mixture of seasoned older players and the young and aspiring with only the sum of their individual ambitions holding the side together. The game itself passed in a bit of a blur and I know that I made mistakes.

The selectors, however, must have seen some promise because I kept my place in the Whites for the final trial a fortnight later.

The fit again Micky Grant was now selected as stand-off for the Whites. At the time he was playing full-back for Harlequins and automatically in the dressing room before the game he put on the number one shirt (under the old numbering system) and I had similarly opted for my normal number six. Fortunately, someone spotted our mistakes before we reached the pitch. The result is of next to no importance in a trial, but the 9–9 draw was a better outcome for the Whites than for the established Blues.

When the team to play France was announced just before Hogmanay 1956, Micky Grant was selected at stand-off and I achieved the first of my ambitions by being chosen at full-back. Also in the team for his first cap was Eddie McKeating. Two years previously we brought in the new year sitting up in an overnight train from London to Edinburgh. The year before, we were in a night club in Toulouse and now we were celebrating our selection at home in Warriston.

With the initial excitement over, it was back to Catterick with an anxious two weeks to pass wrapping myself in cotton wool before the big day in Paris.

FIVE

REALISING A DREAM

The team was announced on Sunday 30 December, the day after the final trial, but I had very little time to celebrate at home. That night I caught the late train back to Darlington, eventually arriving in camp at about 3 a.m. This train from the Waverley was always busy with national servicemen returning to base and was a recurring feature for two years of my life.

My teammates at Catterick were about as excited as I was at my selection and I was allowed to sit out the next match against Halifax. I didn't miss out on my scheduled guard duty however, which meant a night without sleep. With only days to go before running on to the pitch in Paris I was very conscious of taking no risks. In those days a visit to the cinema always finished with the playing of the national anthem and I was very aware that the next time I heard *God Save the Queen* would be seconds before the kick-off at Colombes.

It was back to Edinburgh on the Wednesday in time to fly to Paris the next day with the rest of the team. As the only new caps in the side, Eddie and I were sharing a room in the Hotel Normandy on the Avenue de l'Opera. This was decidedly more comfortable than my Nissen hut in Catterick. In the afternoon we had a bus tour of Paris and in the evening we were taken to the Folies Bergère. By Presbyterian Edinburgh standards of that time it was a very risqué floor show.

On Friday afternoon we had a run-out under the leadership of Jim Greenwood, the captain. I had shared a room once with Ernie Michie playing for the Army but apart from Eddie he was the only other player in the team that I knew. If there was any talk of tactics for the following day they passed me by but it came as a shock to be told by Jim that I would be taking the kicks at goal. I hadn't done any place kicking for any of the representative teams I had played for since leaving school but it didn't seem to be the time for a discussion on the subject, so kicker I was.

The most practical advice I got on the morning of the game was that the plumbing at Colombes was pretty primitive (of the hole in the floor variety) and that all my necessary ablutions should be taken care of before leaving the hotel.

How did I feel now that I was about to achieve my longest-held ambition? My worst fear was that I would find myself completely out of my depth and that I would be letting everyone down, especially family, friends, school teachers and many others who had given me support and encouragement. In my diary for that fateful day I noted that I was not as nervous as I expected to be . . . but all things are relative.

The plumbing at Colombes lived down to its reputation, but the pitch was in very good condition. As the two packs of forwards slugged it out I realised why there had been no real requirement for a tactical plan. Our forwards were absolutely terrific, particularly while covering for hooker Bob McEwan when he was off temporarily for running repairs. The half-backs on both sides took a terrible hammering and I thought that Micky Grant, specially, was very brave under the physical pounding. The back five on both sides were largely spectators, although the wings were regularly employed throwing the ball into the line-out.

What ball did come my way I dealt with, but my touch-kicking was often overly ambitious, a continuing fault, which put unnecessary pressure on the rest of the team.

Midway through the first half we were awarded a penalty about thirty yards out and straight in front of the posts. My first place kick in international rugby rose just high enough to rebound off the crossbar.

There was plenty, therefore, to ponder at half-time, especially as we were now playing into a brisk sleet/snow-laden wind. The forward battle continued unabated and Micky Grant remained heroic behind them when all of a sudden fate intervened.

Jacques Bouquet, the French stand-off, miscued a clearing kick near his own line, the ball missed touch and came bobbling along the ground to me . . . and I dropped a goal. Up to that point, I'd been having a pretty average game – then came this incredible slice of luck which gave my career at that level a badly-needed lift.

I don't mean lucky in the sense that I dropped the goal because that was the result of years of practising at Goldenacre and the ball was between the posts before I had had time to think about it, but it was lucky in that I was presented with the opportunity. In the rest of my career at any level of rugby I can only recall being presented with three other similar situations where dropping a goal was a realistic possibility.

Just for the record, two of these chances were successful. One for the British and Irish Lions against Taranaki in New Zealand in 1959 and the other, co-incidentally, against France at Colombes in 1963. The third was playing in Aberdeen for the North Midlands against Australia – and was unsuccessful. The majority of the drop goals I kicked in senior rugby were from passes from the scrum-half irrespective of the position I was playing.

With my confidence suitably boosted, I kicked a late penalty and the game was won by 6 points to 0.

Despite the language barrier the teams mixed well at the banquet after the match. All sorts of strange drinks were flowing freely and Ian Swan and André Boniface in particular made sure that I got more than my fair share.

The next day, the London edition of the *Sunday Express* printed the following: 'Amid popping corks and good-natured bonhomie, sat a pale-faced, slim-chested young man in a kilt, sipping a pineapple juice, quietly taking in the scene with the casual confident air of one used to dining on the Left Bank six nights a week instead of in a British Army mess.' More accurate headlines could have been, 'Pissed in the Pigalle' or 'Legless at the Lido' but at least that piece of creative journalism did my reputation no harm.

In the Five Nations Championship at that time, there was a three-week gap between fixtures, which were played on a fixed rotation, and meant an immediate return to club matches. In my case, this involved a regimental game in the Army Cup, played at Aldershot, and an Army fixture against the University at Oxford, both at stand-off.

For the next game against Wales at Murrayfield, the forwards were deservedly reselected en bloc, but Micky Grant, who I thought had had a great game in Paris, was dropped. Lack of consistency in selection was generally acknowledged to have been the main reason for Scotland's recent run of seventeen successive defeats. Was this evidence that the selectors had not learned their lesson? The experience of Arthur Dorward at scrum-half is a good example. In the seven seasons from 1950 to 1956 he played eleven games, out of a possible thirty, with six different stand-offs while in 1957 he played in all four games, but with four different partners. It might be argued that the lesson had only been partly learned.

The scene was now set for my first international at Murrayfield. Probably because I hadn't missed a home game as a spectator for the last ten years I was much more nervous than I had been in the relative anonymity of Colombes. The Welsh always travelled with a large and noisy support and the crowd was estimated at 75,000. The game was as hard and as forward-dominated as it had been in Paris but, in much better weather conditions, there was a bit more movement of the ball among the backs. Wales had the elusive Cliff Morgan at stand-off, so they were looking for opportunities to run the ball. From quite an early stage of the game, I had a strong feeling that this was a match we should win. In the end, it took an opportunist drop goal by Arthur Dorward to give us a narrow 9 points to 6 victory. It was also the first season since 1949 that Scotland had won their first two games in the Championship.

The following Saturday, I played for the Royal Signals Catterick in Lancashire against Waterloo and the next Wednesday I was playing for the Army against the Civil Service at Aldershot when I dislocated my shoulder. Under today's laws it would have been an illegal spear tackle as I was picked up and dumped unceremoniously on my shoulder – but back then this was quite within the laws. The bad news was that this happened only ten days before Scotland's next Test against Ireland. The good news was that the Civil Service full-back was a doctor (Gwyn Rowlands) and he immediately put the shoulder joint back in place.

I headed straight back to Edinburgh after the game, hopefully to get some expert treatment for my shoulder. At that time the SRU provided no medical facilities but very fortunately my future father-in-law had played for the Hearts and still had a good enough connection with the club to get me on to the treatment table at Tynecastle.

Also receiving treatment there for a thigh injury was Scotland teammate Tommy McClung, whose father also had a football background. Two days before the Irish game I tried out my shoulder against Tommy's thigh on the pitch at Tynecastle. It was quite a unique situation but probably not the heaviest tackle ever seen at the ground.

After two caps both on the winning side and doing nothing wrong and plenty right, Eddie McKeating was dropped to allow for the introduction of Jimmy Maxwell of Langholm as the third stand-off of the season. It seemed a strange decision to make an unnecessary change in a winning side.

To further prove that my shoulder had healed, the SRU sent me to see an orthopaedic surgeon in his Drumsheugh consulting rooms. After a cursory examination, and having me hang by my injured arm on his consulting room door, I was declared fit.

I'm making light of the injury but in the days before substitutes it was a serious error of judgement to go onto the field carrying an injury. The case of TGH Jackson, a Scottish wing three-quarter, at Twickenham eight years earlier was still cited as an instance of making the wrong decision leaving his team seriously weakened for most of the game.

With my schoolboy hero Jackie Kyle playing at stand-off for Ireland I was expecting my positional play and handling to being severely tested. In that I was not disappointed. To make matters even more difficult, the game was played entirely in a snow storm. I was so cold and numb that I doubt if I would have noticed a repeat dislocation of my shoulder. Also in the Irish side was an old schoolboy opponent, Tony O'Reilly. We had played against each other four times in Heriot's versus Belvedere College matches. Although we were the same age, he was now in his third season of international rugby and with a successful Lions tour to South Africa behind him. He had become the youngest-ever player selected for the Lions and had played on the wing at

Ellis Park in Johannesburg against the Springboks before a then world-record crowd of 95,000, scoring a try in a famous 23–22 Lions victory.

Our match at Murrayfield wasn't nearly as impressive a setting, as the game was almost completely dominated by the weather and the outside backs were virtual spectators as a result.

With Jim Greenwood out injured, our pack came off second best and, scoring the only try of the match Ireland won by 5 points to 3. In my three games so far, with scoring being low, the side whose pack shaded the forward battle on the day ended up on the winning side.

This was proved without doubt in the final international of the season against England at Twickenham. In the process they scored three tries in a 16–3 victory. The England team that day was, I consider, the best that I ever played against. The front row of George Hastings, Eric Evans, the captain, and Ron Jacobs was rock solid, the second row of David Marques and John Currie was the classic combination of jumper and enforcer, and the back row of Reg Higgins, Alan Ashcroft and Peter Robbins were ahead of their time as constructive ball-players.

In the backs, Dickie Jeeps at scrum-half and Peter Jackson, Jeff Butterfield and Phil Davies in the three-quarter line were all world-class players. Bob Challis, at full-back, was a newcomer, but stand-off Ricky Bartlett and winger Peter Thompson were both highly experienced players.

With the number of players at their disposal, England should always be strong, but it is only when they are consistent in selection and well led that they really pull their weight. The 1957 team captained by Eric Evans was a prime example and has been followed by captains Bill Beaumont, Will Carling and Martin Johnson.

Apart from the four internationals in the first four months of 1957, I played another ten games and six sevens tournaments, all at stand-off. Taking into account all the games, two were in Catterick and Paris, three at Aldershot, Murrayfield and Twickenham, with single visits to Oxford, Liverpool, Melrose, Hawick, Bradford, Huddersfield and Langholm. During that sequence of games, the Army won the Inter-Services Championship, 1TR Royal Signals won the Northern Command and Army Cups and Heriot's FP won the Melrose Sevens.

As players tend to be their own sternest critics, how did I think I performed overall in the four internationals? My worst fear of being totally out of my depth was, fortunately, not realised. In the modern game full-backs and wingers are more or less interchangeable, but in the immediate post-war years, full-backs and stand-offs were seen as requiring the same basic skills. My fielding throughout was consistent, though not flawless, and my touch-kicking improved after a poor start in Paris, though I continued to be over ambitious to get length – much to the annoyance of the forwards.

It is probably worth making the point that irrespective of the position I was playing in any particular game, I always thought like a stand-off. Whichever side won possession, I was always trying to work out the options and to anticipate the next move.

Much was made in the press that I had scored in every game. By today's standard one penalty a game would be seen as a trivial return. However, in the 1950s fewer infringements resulted in penalties being awarded so opportunities were limited. Even with that qualification, I would not give my place-kicking more than half marks.

SIX

CITY OF PERSPIRING DREAMS

With time now fast running out, I was beginning to be seriously concerned about my ability to pass the Latin exam needed to get into Cambridge. I had an interview with the Regimental Commanding Officer who was sympathetic to my problem and he agreed that I would not be selected for any cricket matches which entailed time away from camp. Nevertheless, that was a big disappointment as I had really enjoyed the Inter-Corps matches the previous season – but needs must.

This sympathy did not extend to the Regimental Sergeant Major, who now took great delight in ensuring that, belatedly, I did some soldiering. By this time, I had a second stripe and I was ordered to take part in the Queen's Birthday Parade and a visit by the Duke of Edinburgh, both of which required innumerable rehearsals. He also sent me to help organise a week's exercise under canvas on the Yorkshire Moors.

During April and May, I spent all my spare time studying and in mid-June I went to Cambridge to sit the entrance exam. I didn't feel that I had done enough to pass and within a few days that was confirmed. Further enquiries showed that I had one last chance to sit the exam.

FROM J. M. K. VYVYAN
TUTOR

TRINITY COLLEGE
CAMBRIDGE
TEL. 58201

3rd July, 1957.

Dear Scotland,

I have now seen your marks in the Previous
Examination. They show that you were not very far off
passing in the first paper but that you did very poorly
indeed in the second paper. However, your Headmaster
has explained to me that you did the second paper the
wrong way as a result of misleading instructions in the
past, so I think it is just worth while your taking the
examination again at the beginning of October and I am
accordingly entering you for it. If you pass you will
be allowed to come into residence and I am putting you
provisionally on the list of freshmen. But if you should
fail you will not be able to remain up so you may decide
not to settle yourself in very definitely when coming up
for the examination, although you will be allotted rooms
as if regularly admitted to the College.

Yours sincerely,

23173022 L/Cpl. K.J.F. Scotland,
Technical Stores,
2 Squadron, 1 Training Regt.,
Royal Signals,
Catterick Camp,
Yorks.

I immediately applied for an early demob. The situation was complicated by the current Suez Crisis and rumours of National Service being extended, but after much indecision I was eventually allowed to leave the Army at the end of July, a month ahead of schedule. This allowed me two months to improve my Latin.

My chances of success were greatly enhanced when I was taken under the wing of the retired Rector of Edinburgh Academy, A L F Smith. Mr Smith was a regular worshipper at St Mary's Cathedral and was known to my father. He was a classical scholar and it was a rare privilege to be tutored by someone of his standing. He was reliably reputed to have turned down the headmastership of Eton during his time at the Academy.

Being back in Edinburgh allowed me to see a lot more of Doreen and enabled me to start the new rugby season with Heriot's. For the first time in my life, I was actually involved in fitness training. At school, our life style had been such that fitness was taken for granted and we had played practice games twice a week, usually finishing up with ten minutes of football. The situation at Catterick was similar and when we did have time to practise we spent time on moves rather than fitness training.

In September, I played my one and only game for Edinburgh, but the highlight was the traditional early-season fixture against Hawick at Goldenacre. It was a game which always attracted a capacity crowd and, as a schoolboy, I had been an avid, and partial, spectator. A win by 6 points to 5 was an indication of the intensity in which the game was played and kept the capacity partisan crowd involved until the very end.

On 30 September, an eight-hour train journey to Cambridge, with changes at Newcastle, Peterborough and Ely, set me up for my Entrance Exam the following day.

This time I was much better prepared, thanks particularly to Mr Smith, but I had to endure a fraught five days before I got the news that I had passed.

I am not by nature a worrier, but I was tormented by the thought that failure in the exam would mean packing up my bags and beating an ignominious retreat to Edinburgh. The number of people I felt I would be letting down grew by the day as I contemplated the result of failure.

The news that I had passed and that I could now begin to lead the life of a normal undergraduate naturally came as a great relief. However, it was as though worrying had become a habit. I started to doubt whether or not I would be selected for the forthcoming Freshers' Trial. On the face of it, that was totally ridiculous, but I think it was an indication of how fragile my self-confidence had become.

In fact, when the teams were announced, I was chosen at full-back to captain the senior side. Instead of banishing my negative thoughts this merely seemed to compound them. A combination of 'Heriot's boys don't go to Cambridge' and failing to get a commission during National Service came back to bite me, leaving me woefully short of confidence.

My first-ever trial at school as a ten-year-old I described as being surrounded by headless chickens. This time I was the headless chicken and the outcome was undoubtedly the worst game of rugby that I had ever played at any level in my life. In the space of eighty minutes I had gone from being an international to, at best, third choice full-back for Cambridge.

I had certainly never assumed that I would walk into the university team. In fact, because of my preoccupation with the Latin exam, I had given little thought to either day to day life in Cambridge or how university rugby was organised. I was impressed that Bill Downey, the university captain, whom I had never met, took the trouble to seek me out to tell me that I would not be selected for the next game. He explained that David Millard, the previous year's full-back, was back for another year and was the man in possession. After the trial I was definitely also behind Alan Prosser-Harries, an experienced Welshman from Llanelli. With brutal honesty he told me that opportunities might arise but with only eight weeks until the game against Oxford, they were not guaranteed.

With all the benefits of hindsight, it was probably a good thing that I did not immediately get absorbed into the intensity of university rugby. As I was to discover later, the whole of the first term up to the game against Oxford in early December was more or less totally devoted to playing and thinking about rugby.

It gave me a chance to settle into a more normal and balanced undergraduate life. I bought a gown and a second-hand bicycle, which were both essentials for life in Cambridge. Through the Freshers Trial I met Dave MacSweeney and Frank Booth, who both became close friends throughout our time at university and beyond. It also meant that I had time to integrate fully into college life at Trinity.

A meeting with my tutor established that I would be studying for a degree in economics and a subsequent meeting with my director of studies outlined what that would entail. The format for any arts degree was similar – three or four lectures every morning were followed by preparation for a weekly tutorial. The norm was to prepare an essay on a given topic and have it discussed with my tutor, usually with one other student in attendance.

With my academic timetable now under way, I could take stock of the rugby options. The university ran two teams, the Blues and the LX Club, each playing two games a week up until their fixtures against Oxford at the end of term. Trinity College Rugby Club also had a largely mid-week fixture list against other colleges.

During October, I played three games for the college with one call-up for the LX Club. At that point, London Scottish came to my rescue and invited me to travel to play for them on

Saturdays. This looked like a good solution for me and I duly played for them at Richmond against Bedford. The following week I was again selected to play at Richmond this time against . . . Cambridge University. It was not to be, however. Because of injuries I was claimed by the university and I ended up in the unusual position of appearing in the programme for one side but actually playing for the opposition.

I really appreciated the effort that London Scottish made to give me the opportunity to play first-class rugby, but it did not work out. For the rest of the term, because of injuries, I played regularly for the LX Club with one further game for the Blues. Not that these games affected my overall position in the full-back pecking order because I was not selected for either of the sides to play Oxford – then, however, an injury again intervened. David Millard pulled out of the game at Twickenham which allowed Allan Prosser-Harries to get his Blue and I played for the LX Club at Oxford against the Oxford Greyhounds.

After a fairly traumatic start, I was now feeling comfortable with life at Cambridge. I had a good circle of friends both within college and throughout the rest of the university. The discipline of regular morning lectures and flexible afternoon or evening studying suited me well. In rugby terms, I had thoroughly enjoyed all the games that I had played and I had banished any negative thoughts. However, it was odd to realise that for the first time in my career I was being considered solely as a full-back.

Back home for Christmas, I played at full-back for the senior side in the first Scottish trial, largely without incident. The following Saturday, I played in the centre for Heriot's against Melville College FP and picked up a leg injury which was bad enough to force me to call off from the final trial.

Had I played in the final trial without making any obvious mistakes, I think I would probably have done just about enough to keep my place in the Scotland team. This wasn't to be, however, and I was dropped for the first time.

Back in Cambridge in January, it was like the start of a new season. The build-up for the next game against Oxford in December started immediately and only those who were expected to be available at the end of the year were considered for selection. With both David Millard and Allan Prosser-Harries leaving in June, I was now in pole position. I found the new captain, Geoff Windsor-Lewis, very supportive and I was able to secure a regular place in the team.

Meanwhile, having missed two games completely, I was included as a travelling reserve by Scotland for a home game against Australia and the away trip to Dublin for the Irish Five Nations game. Robin Chisholm, who had regained the full-back position, suffered a nasty head injury in Dublin and could not be considered for the final fixture of 1958 against England. His misfortune was my gain and I was chosen for the last match of the season against England at Murrayfield. Considering that England had twelve of the team that had comprehensively beaten us 16–3 the previous year, the 3–3 result was, on paper, an improvement – but my brief diary entry at the time 'All over England in the Calcutta Cup' indicated that it was a game that we could have won.

The season ended with a tour to France with Cambridge, taking in Toulon, Nice and Paris and being selected by the Barbarians for their Easter tour to South Wales, where I played against Cardiff, Swansea and Newport. A clash with my first-year exams prevented me accepting an invitation to go on a short summer tour to South Africa with the Barbarians.

When I returned to Edinburgh for what remained of the Easter holidays, I had a decision to make. Would I cut the holidays even shorter by returning to Cambridge to take part in the trial for the cricket team, known as 'Freshers' Nets'?

Early in my time at Trinity, I had discussed with my tutor, who thought I had more chance of getting a cricket rather than a rugby Blue, how it was possible to play cricket six days a week in the summer term and still get a degree. He cited the example of the well-known England cricketer, P B H May, who had got up at 5.30 every morning and did his day's work before appearing at Fenners, the university cricket ground. I did give that suggestion a try, but unfortunately by six o'clock I had gone back to sleep.

I was also aware that the previous year's wicketkeeper, Australian Brian Swift, was still available and taking a line through my rugby experience I realised that I was very unlikely to make a quick breakthrough. As it happened, before the season started Brian Swift was tragically killed in a car accident and it was a freshman, Chris Howland, who took his place. Chris also became an LX Club full-back and we became close friends. He ended up as Captain of Cricket at the same time as I was Captain of Rugby.

Deep down I knew that it was wishful thinking to imagine that I could play virtually full-time cricket and pass my first-year degree exams, so my cricket ambitions had to be put on hold.

The consolation of spending that time in Edinburgh was seeing more of Doreen and ending the rugby season by retaining the Melrose Sevens Cup with the same Heriot's team of Jimmy Weir, Eddie McKeating, myself, Drew Ramsay, Dave Syme, Bob Tollervey and David Edwards. In the semi-final, we beat an all-international Co-optimists seven of Arthur Smith, Tony O'Reilly, Donald Scott, Andy Mulligan, Douglas Elliot, Karl Mullen and Ronnie Kavanagh. They had pace aplenty, but with their veteran forwards running out of steam the old adage that possession is nine-tenths of the law in sevens helped us to a narrow victory.

Although important exams were only six weeks away, life in the summer term seemed somehow more relaxed. Long warm evenings wandering on the 'Backs' or even the occasional attempt at punting on the Cam were a pleasant contrast to the often cold and damp days of winter. I spent a lot of time on revision, but still managed about three games of cricket a week as well as fitting in some spectating at Fenners. Most of my cricket was for Trinity, but I played a few games for the Crusaders. The Crusaders was the nearest thing that the university had to a 2nd XI, but in fact it was more a question of availability than being part of a side picked on merit.

During the term I was elected a member of the Hawks Club, which became my second home for the rest of my time at Cambridge. Membership of the Hawks was confined more or less to students who had become Blues across the complete range of sports. My proposer was Trinity wing-forward Richard Scott, who in later life became well-known as Lord Scott of the 1992 Scott Enquiry into the export of defence equipment to Iraq.

After the exams were over, Doreen paid her first visit to Cambridge where, as well as attending an atmospheric cocktail party in the college gardens, we went to the Christ's May Ball with my new friends Frank Booth and Dave MacSweeney and their partners.

Back in Edinburgh in the second week in June for a 'Long Vacation' of nearly four months, my first priority was to have an operation to remove a piece of bone from my right elbow. It didn't completely stop me playing cricket or doing much else, but it was very painful when I straightened my arm. The operation was performed by Mr Saville at the Princess Margaret Rose Hospital in Edinburgh on 23 June and by 2 July the stitches were out – the next day I was back playing cricket.

Just before and just after the operation, I had had scores in the 80s but I was truly astounded to be picked to play cricket for Scotland against Ireland as a batsman. I did have pretensions as a wicketkeeper but Jimmy Brown of Perthshire had that position well sewn up. The Scotland v Ireland game is played over three days and is treated as a first-class fixture and, as such, players get a mention in the annual edition of Wisden, cricket's bible. That turned out to be my only consolation.

The game was played in Ayr and the three days were reduced to one and a half by rain. In my one innings I faced three balls, none of which I managed to touch, and on the third one I was out stumped.

To put a positive spin on my selection, our twelfth man that day, still a schoolboy, was Mike Denness who went on to have a stellar career as an England cricketer.

The game was scheduled for Saturday, Monday and Tuesday. The Sunday was both free and dry and I enjoyed my first visit to Prestwick golf club, which has become one of my favourite golf courses and golf clubs, both of which retain an old-fashioned elegance.

In August, I did two weeks as a relief driver in Fife and the Lothians making deliveries for a wholesale chemist and helping out at home with some painter-work. Another two weeks were spent in St Andrews on a caravanning/golfing holiday with the Edwards twins, David and George. We played thirty-six holes a day, mainly on the Eden, but also had the thrill of playing the Old Course for the first time. For the first week, Doreen was also in St Andrews on a family holiday so we were able to spend lots of time together.

*

Before heading back to Cambridge in early October for my second year, the 1958/59 rugby season had got off to a hectic start. As well as playing three games for Heriot's, including the traditional opener against Hawick at Goldenacre, I had played at Twickenham for London Scottish and made two separate trips to play in Cornwall, one of them being a pre-season university tour.

Although I had managed to pass my first-year economics exams, with third-class honours, I had found much of the course much too mathematical for my liking and ability. Economic history, and the lectures of Prof A J Youngson, had been the highlight of my first year and, with the agreement of my tutor, I changed to study modern European history for the second part of my tripos.

Domestically, I remained in Whewells Court, where my first-year digs had been, but I was now sharing rooms with Graham Hornett, a hockey Blue and an enthusiastic timpanist in the university orchestra. Our rooms overlooked the entrance to the Hawks Club in All Saints Passage. The window, however, was heavily barred to stop us, or anyone else for that matter, using it to climb in and break the 10.00 p.m. college curfew. The Hawks Club was an excellent place for meeting a wide variety of students from across the university, covering all sports for which a Blue or Half-Blue was awarded and, as I have said, it became the social centre of my life for the remainder of my time in Cambridge.

A year on from my disastrous Freshers' Trial, I was now fairly well established as number one choice at full-back, but I continued to think like a stand-off. In fact, throughout my entire rugby career I always saw the game through the eyes of a stand-off. During my second season at Catterick a young Welshman from Newbridge, Gethin Evans, straight from the 'Welsh fly-half factory', I joined the regiment. My seniority as a corporal meant that I continued to play stand-off with Gethin expressing his talents at full-back. As a team, we worked at moves bringing Gethin into the game, mainly trying to find ways to exploit a generous blindside. Now, in a different environment, and with my role reversed as the (somewhat unwilling) full-back, it just naturally evolved that I should look for ways to add something extra to the team's attack.

*

By the mid 1950s rugby union was changing. From the twenty-a-side hacking game of the late 19th century, rugby had evolved, and grown in popularity to become, through the 1920s and 1930s a major international spectator sport. The early domination by the forwards had changed to a more balanced game where backs and forwards shared equal prominence.

With enthusiasm for rugby rekindled after the Second World War, and with players returning from the Services, it was natural the game continued to be played in the 1930s pattern. In fact, it took almost a decade before new ideas were introduced.

The forwards were there to win the ball. The first priority of the half-backs was to put the ball into the opposition half of the pitch, where, when the forwards next won possession, the ball would be passed along the three-quarter line. Given sufficient possession, the idea was that each of the backs would have a go at beating his opposite number in the hope of finding a soft spot which could then be exploited. The full-back was very much the last line of defence being expected to catch, kick and, occasionally tackle.

The above is a bit of a simplification of the way the game was approached, but not much. Individual teams would play to their own strengths and weaknesses and would adjust their tactics accordingly, but within the above framework.

With rugby matches on TV a novelty even in the late 1950s, and video analysis as yet undreamed of, it took some time before new ideas were absorbed into the game. I first became aware of new thinking while I was in Catterick doing National Service. The innovator was David Onllwyn Brace, a Welsh scrum-half at Oxford. From a scrum in the middle of the field, he had his stand-off and two centres positioned in such a way that when he got possession, the opposition could not be sure who would be first receiver. A simple idea, but one that kept the opposition on the back foot. In conjunction with scissor and dummy-scissor movements, these ideas became integrated into the game. So it was that, with new attacking formations in mind, we began to experiment with using the full-back as an attacking force.

To do so at that time required two things. It needed a back division which bought into the idea and plenty of time to put moves into practice. At Cambridge we had the opportunity – Oxford were probably the only other first-class club in Britain at that time who also trained in daylight – and Geoff Windsor-Lewis our captain and centre wholeheartedly embraced the concept.

The first move we practised was the full-back coming into the three-quarter line outside the outside centre aiming to create the classic two-on-one situation. It was called either from a line-out or a scrum close to one touchline. The move was called regularly in these early games, but only rarely executed. With no such thing then as a miss pass, the ball had to go quickly and accurately through four pairs of hands before any possible advantage could arise, so it could be wasteful of hard-won possession. When everything clicked, we scored tries from the move and the principle of creating an overlap worked well enough to encourage me to use the idea, but in open play rather than in a set-piece situation.

Although it quickly fell out of favour as a set piece move, coming into the line outside the outside centre remained my favourite point of attack. To work, all the players on the inside had to commit their opposite numbers by straightening the line as they passed and I had to inject some pace onto the ball. I found it interesting that in practice with three-quarter lines of varying abilities, I had to struggle to even keep pace with them, while in a game situation their collective line speed was slower and I could usually manage to increase the pace on the ball. It is worth labouring the point that coming into the line to create an overlap only works with an injection of pace.

During October and November, concentration on rugby, and the game against Oxford in particular, was all-consuming. The weekly pattern was to train on a Monday, have tea together on the Tuesday, play a match on the Wednesday, train on the Thursday, tea on the Friday and play a match on Saturday. Sunday was a day of rest. The fixture list was demanding and during that period included the top Welsh clubs Cardiff and Newport, strong Midland sides Bedford, Coventry, Leicester, and Northampton, and Harlequins, Richmond and London Scottish from London, climaxing with a game against an international select XV raised by Micky Steele-Bodger. As an aside, before Micky sadly passed away in May 2019, he had managed to raise a team to play against the university for more than seventy years – a feat surely worthy of a place in the *Guinness Book of Records*.

With my studies now covering modern European history from the Renaissance, British constitutional history from 1688, the 19th century expansion of Europe, theories of the modern state and the Anglo-Irish problems of 1916-23, time-management became important. In this respect, I had an ideal role model in my Scottish international colleague, Arthur Smith. In a Cambridge where students had an ambition either to gain a first-class degree, a Blue, a regular girlfriend or indeed just be one of the boys, Arthur managed to achieve all four. Apart, obviously, from being multi-talented, he was a master at organising and using his time.

The preparation for, and the build-up to, the game against Oxford in early December was much more intense than anything I had previously experienced. At school and in the army, I had spent a lot of time practising individual and, to some extent, team skills, but had never done any systematic training. After eight weeks of focus on all three, I was fitter than I had ever been and was now surrounded by players who knew exactly what was expected of them and who had confidence in each other.

In the Cambridge side chosen to play stand-off against Oxford was another Scottish internationalist, Gordon Waddell. We had first played together, successfully, at the end of 1954 for London Scottish Schoolboys against our Richmond counterparts and the more I played with Gordon the more I came to appreciate his skill and tactical ability.

During our three seasons at Cambridge, we played off each other in open play with either scissors or dummy scissors in much the same way as Gerald Davies and JPR Williams did for Wales a decade later.

The game itself, played in front of a capacity crowd at Twickenham, was a very convincing win for Cambridge. Our forwards were outstanding and the backs, controlled with authority by Gordon, scored four tries. This was the first time since the 1930s that a team had scored four tries in the Varsity Match. I also had the personal satisfaction of creating an overlap from full-back for one of the tries. While everyone in the team played to their limits, the leadership of our captain, Geoff Windsor-Lewis, both during the game and, more importantly, through the long build-up, could not be overestimated.

SEVEN

THE ROAR OF THE LIONS

'New Zealand is the Mecca of all rugby men and a tour there is the greatest honour, and experience, that comes a player's way in the Home Countries.' So wrote the respected *Sunday Times* rugby correspondent, Vivian Jenkins.

Adding interest to the 1959 Five Nations was the impending summer tour of the British and Irish Lions to Australia, New Zealand and Canada. Early in the New Year, I, and many others, were asked, if selected, would we be available to travel. As the tour was due to last nearly five months, this was a decision that very few could take lightly.

I was in the fortunate position that I had no exams to sit that summer, but my director of studies explained that as I would miss the entire summer term I would have to add on an extra term the following autumn. Fortunately, the Alexander Cross Trustees saw no problem in deferring my grant a further term, so I was happy to throw my hat into the selection mix.

Playing for the Lions was not something that I had previously thought much about. My childhood ambition of playing rugby for Scotland had never extended to the Lions. I had been aware of, and read about, the 1950 tour to New Zealand and the 1955 tour to South Africa, but with little personal contact. I had the vicarious pleasure of having played as a schoolboy against Tony O'Reilly, who was one of the 1955 stars, and on Army duty I had shared a room with Ernie Michie on his return from the same tour, but that was about it. Suddenly, seemingly from out of nowhere, arose the possibility of becoming a Lion.

Taking selectorial whims out of the equation, the squad would be likely to comprise of thirty players made up of two players for each position. Therefore, all other things being equal, anyone playing regularly for Scotland, England, Ireland or Wales during the 1959 season had a 50/50 chance of being selected for the tour. Quite early on I knew that two likely Scots, Arthur Smith and Hamish Kemp, were not available to travel, but I had no clue about availability from any of the other countries.

By the start of 1959, I was fitter than I had ever been and for the first half of the season had been playing regularly at full-back in a consistently high standard of rugby for a successful team trying hard to play as varied a game as possible. As a result, for the first time I felt comfortable with the thought of playing international rugby and being able to make a positive contribution.

As always, our first game of the 1959 Five Nations was against France early in the New Year at Stade Colombes in Paris. Any overconfidence I might have been feeling soon evaporated as it turned out to be the most one-sided international I ever had the misfortune to play in. The game was played almost entirely in our twenty-five and it was only by some heroic tackling combined with a generous share of luck that France were confined to one try and two drop goals in their 9–0 victory.

The Scottish selectors, or the Big Five as they were generally known, decided that the performance was so dismal that they would hold an unscheduled extra trial before the next game. Consequently, on the Saturday before the Welsh match, the usual forty or so hopefuls assembled for lunch at the North British Hotel in Edinburgh. Unfortunately, this predated Murrayfield's electric blanket and the only frost-free pitch available was in Ayr, a good two hours' drive away. It probably turned out to be a worthwhile exercise if only to get the defeat in Paris out of our systems. In truth, we probably should not have been so despondent because it transpired that France were at the start of a good run which saw them dominate the Five Nations for the next four seasons.

In the rest of our matches we beat Wales 6–5, lost 8–3 to Ireland, and drew 3–3 with England at Twickenham. All very tightly contested games with a total of only three tries scored – so not a feast of open running rugby.

As the season progressed, and with Lions selection in mind, it was obvious that Terry Davies would go as first-choice full-back. Ireland played Noel Henderson, a veteran and successful centre from the 1950 tour to New Zealand, out of position at full-back and although he generally played well, I felt he would not be considered. With the touring party to be announced just days after the Calcutta Cup was played, it appeared that the second full-back would be either Jim Hetherington of England or myself.

Jim had got a Blue at Cambridge in 1955 and had played regularly thereafter for Northampton, but was in his first season playing for England. I suppose that if either of us had had an outstanding game that would have been crucial, but I think in the end it was small things that went in my favour. I am sure that in the selectors' eyes, my attacking potential was a plus but my defence was a negative. As it turned out, I was able to make two fairly crucial tackles towards the end of the Calcutta Cup to perhaps dispel their doubts.

Without in any way taking anything for granted, I was quietly confident that I would be selected. A few years after the tour

I bumped into Jim walking along Kings Road in Chelsea and in the course of conversation he told me that he too had been pretty confident of selection and had been very disappointed not to be chosen. Roughly sixteen months after being third-choice full-back at Cambridge, I had indeed been the lucky one.

There were two selectors from each country under the chairmanship of the previously announced manager, a Scot, Alf Wilson, and the chosen squad, under the captaincy of Irish hooker, Ronnie Dawson, consisted of nine Irish, nine Welsh, eight English and four Scots. The most obvious selectorial whim was picking an equal balance of fifteen backs and fifteen forwards with a utility back being chosen at the expense of a back-row forward. The selectors also showed their independence by picking two Englishmen, scrum-half Dickie Jeeps and wing-forward Peter Robbins, who had not played for England during the current season.

There was a gap of seven weeks between selection and meeting together at Eastbourne for a week's training and we were asked to play as little rugby as possible during that time. I was already committed to the Barbarians' Easter tour to south Wales and a university trip for three games in France. I played five games without mishap but Peter Robbins was not so lucky. Sitting in the stand at Newport, I actually heard the crack of Peter's leg being broken, which at any time is a distressing experience but knowing that was the end of his ambition to play for the Lions was truly sickening. With no chance of recovering in time Peter was replaced by Ken Smith from Kelso, adding another Scot to the party.

*

By Easter 1959, Doreen and I had been an item, not that the phrase had yet been coined, for five years. While I was still a student, Doreen was now a qualified teacher of domestic science. For most of that time, we only met during my short visits to Edinburgh, supplemented by regular letters and occasional telephone calls. Lengthy absences became more common once I went to Cambridge and would then be away for a whole term. Highlights away from Edinburgh were going to a May Ball in Cambridge and the University Match Ball at the Festival Hall in London in 1958, and another ball in London after the 1959 Calcutta Cup.

With a five-month separation looming, we spent an idyllic week together at Brodick on the Isle of Arran. With the weather gods being kind, we cycled, played golf and explored the island. Little did we realise that twenty-six years later, we would return to live on the island working for the National Trust for Scotland at Brodick Castle.

We had no doubt that we would marry just as soon as we possibly could, but that still looked distant. We did talk then of becoming engaged but my parents, especially my mother, were very strongly against the idea. My parents had saved to buy a house before they were married and felt that, as I was still a student with no income, it was premature to be getting engaged. As I was still living at home and was still financially dependent on them, I took the softer option of following their wishes.

*

1959 was still the in the era of the long Lions tour. Our itinerary comprised six games in Australia, including two Tests, twenty-five in New Zealand, including four Tests, and two games in Canada on our return journey. The overall length of the tour was just short of five months. Of the previous five tours visiting Australia and New Zealand, only the very first Lions visit in 1888 involved more than the thirty-three games scheduled for 1959.

Their total of thirty-five games was matched by the 1966 tour, since when the number of games played has steadily declined to the ten in the 2017 itinerary to New Zealand and eight in the 2021 itinerary to South Africa.

Prior to leaving the UK, we spent an intensive week training together as a squad in Eastbourne. For all but the Scots in the party this was their first introduction to our manager, Alf Wilson. His only travelling support was Ossie Glasgow, secretary to the touring party, an Ulsterman and a former international referee. They were a good combination. Alf could be quite fiery and outspoken while Ossie was a laid back, placid, pipe-smoking smoother of ruffled feathers. Ossie probably had more direct dealings with the players as he weekly handed out our expenses of 10 shillings a day and packets of cigarettes to anyone who was interested. There weren't many smokers but one or two took them because, like being in jail, they were a form of currency.

In response to any query, Ossie's reply was always 'Don't ask me, I'm only the secretary.' This soon became a catchphrase on tour.

Ossie also had a reputation as a bridge player and he taught enough of us the basics of the Acol system which helped us to pass the time on journeys, especially on railcars in the North Island of New Zealand.

In Eastbourne we were presented with our two tour blazers, one for dress occasions and one for everyday wear, and we were also given two Lions ties. Apart from our playing kit, which had been sent ahead to Melbourne, all our other clothing and training kit we provided ourselves. It was a widely held view that had it not been for the extreme amateur position held by the Irish and Scottish unions, more uniform clothing would have been issued.

We had further medical and dental checks. We were told

that we were expected to look smart, be punctual, polite and courteous at all times. No meals were to be taken in rooms. We were to choose from the Table d'Hote Menu and that no alcoholic drinks were to be ordered with meals.

At our first team meeting, we were left in no doubt that we were not going on an extended holiday. Our primary aim was to win but to win playing attractive running rugby. This second point seemed to be made more in hope than expectation as the season's Five Nations matches between all the Home Countries had averaged just over one try per game

Most of us had not trained for over a month, in fact we had been encouraged to rest, so getting fit again was vital. As he had done in South Africa in 1955, Jeff Butterfield who was a trained PE teacher, took our twice-daily sessions. Suffice to say that for the first two days just climbing the stairs to our bedrooms became a painful exercise.

We broke new ground by being the first Lions team to fly to New Zealand. Travelling by sea the 1950 party took thirty-two days to reach their destination. Long-haul flying, however, was still a thing of the future and having set off from London at 1 p.m. on 16 May and after refuelling stops at Zurich, Beirut, Karachi, Calcutta, Bangkok, Singapore and Darwin, we eventually arrived in Melbourne at 5.30 a.m. on 19 May.

To illustrate that touring was not all about playing rugby, by the time we got to bed that night we had attended two official receptions. As we changed location thirty-seven times during the nearly five months of the tour, and as nearly every change seemed to require an official reception, we attended, always properly dressed, but not always willingly. Alf Wilson had warned us in Eastbourne that he was not an enthusiastic or fluent speaker and that if he found himself short of the right word he would often just say 'bugger'. Needless to say, in the course of his many speeches we heard many 'buggers'.

The three days we had to acclimatise before the first game against Victoria were a good opportunity to take stock of my teammates for the next few months. The most influential group were those who had toured with the Lions previously. Malcolm Thomas was the one survivor from the 1950 tour and he did his best to explain what we could expect from rucking in New Zealand. At that time, rucking was virtually unknown in the northern hemisphere. I say 'tried to explain', and I quote from my diary following the game against Auckland: 'One of the hardest games I have ever played in. I was caught in one "ruck" and felt as though I was underneath a stampede of cattle.' Not easy to describe unless you have been there – and an experience I did my very best not to repeat.

The survivors from the 1955 tour to South Africa, Jeff Butterfield, Dickie Jeeps, Hugh McLeod, Bryn Meredith, Tony O'Reilly and Rhys Williams, were all hugely experienced internationalists and in their own different ways helped to mould us into a happy united touring party.

To balance all that experience, I had my twenty-third birthday on tour and eleven of the squad were the same age or younger. We had an acronym for the way we wanted to play – SPEED. Amplified by Ronnie Dawson, the tour captain, this stood for Spirit, Possession, Endurance, Effort and Defence.

All the above made Ronnie's position particularly daunting. Without even having the moral support of a nominated vice-captain, and with appointed coaches still some way in the future, Ronnie was in a very exposed position. That he performed so well deserves huge credit. He led from the front both on and off the field and any success that we had either as a cohesive group socially or as a rugby team was largely down to his unstinting efforts. It was very much a player-driven tour. There was the manager, the secretary and the guy looking after the bags – but on the field it was Ronnie Dawson and the senior players who decided our tactics. The management had a say in selection, but they never appeared on the practice ground or anything like that. The team who were playing the next game would have a run-out, that was basically led by whomever was captain that day.

The highlight of my stay in Melbourne was to be part of a small group given a conducted tour of the Melbourne Cricket Ground by Ian Johnston, a former Australian Test cricket captain. The ground had a capacity of 100,000 and during the winter it was home for the local Australian Rules Football Club. At home, our cricket squares were roped off during the winter. In Melbourne, the square was just part of the football pitch and all it needed between seasons was a heavy roller to make it fit for Test cricket.

Another local institution I experienced was the 'six o'clock swill'. The local pubs were only open for an hour each evening so there was an almost manic necessity to drink quickly. Little glasses called ponies were lined up along the bar and filled with beer from a hose. Then all of a sudden, the locals would appear and go: wallop, wallop, wallop, wallop – and they'd get as many of them down as they could before the bar closed an hour later.

It was quite a relief to eventually get a game under our belts. Victoria were expected to be the weakest side we would play in Australia and at 6 points down to them after quarter of an hour it was not looking good. After this slow start, the forwards began to provide good ball and we eventually scored ten tries in a 53–18 victory. I thoroughly enjoyed the experience of playing behind a back division with the speed, skill and elusiveness of Dickie Jeeps, Bev Risman, Peter Jackson, Jeff Butterfield, David Hewitt and John Young.

The next stop was Sydney to play the strongest of the provincial sides, New South Wales. Our hotel at Coogee Bay was well situated close to the beach. At every change of hotel, we had a change of roommate. This time I shared a large room with John Faull and Bill Mulcahy. We had training facilities within walking distance of the hotel and on the way back we went into the sea for a swim. The locals thought we were mad going in for a swim in mid-winter but they obviously had no experience of the temperature of the North Sea even at its very warmest.

Everyone who was fit and hadn't played in Melbourne was selected for this game. Very sadly for Niall Brophy his tour as a player lasted less than five minutes without him ever touching the ball. In turning to chase a ball kicked behind him, something he must have done a thousand times without any problem, he twisted an ankle so badly that there was no chance of recovery before the end of the tour. It was a good and exciting game to watch but the handicap of playing a man short for most of the game proved too much and we lost 18–14. We were obviously disappointed to lose our unbeaten record so early in the tour, but Jeff Butterfield was philosophical and argued that there were benefits in not carrying that as a burden later in the tour. On the less philosophical side, he also introduced us to drinking games which helped us to drown our sorrows in record-breaking time.

On the Sunday after the game, we saw a bit of Sydney before catching an overnight sleeper to Brisbane. We arrived about midday, went to the inevitable reception and then after dark we went out for a practice session. The reason that our programme seemed out of sequence was that the game the following day was due to be played under floodlights which, for most of us, would be a new experience.

With the first Test against the Wallabies due on Saturday, Tony O'Reilly, Mick English and Stan Coughtrie, who had not yet played in Australia, were included in the team. This meant that everyone, apart from Gordon Waddell who was still in Cambridge sitting his first-year exams, would have had an opportunity to stake a claim for inclusion in the Test team.

I found that I soon forgot that the game was being played under artificial light and as we beat Queensland 39–11, scoring seven tries, the rest of the team must have reacted similarly.

After training the following day, the team for the first Test was announced and I had been selected. Was I delighted? Obviously. Was I surprised? Yes and no. Of the three games played so far, I had been selected for the two easier games and Terry Davies for the New South Wales game, which was considered almost the equivalent of a third Test. Terry had the experience. On the other hand, I had scored a try against Victoria and two against Queensland and had staked my claim.

The game itself was disappointing. The temperature in the shade was over 70, the pitch was brick-hard and there was a lack of the atmosphere normally associated with an international match. It was a game we had to win to give us the credibility we needed before arriving in New Zealand, so we were happy enough with the final score of 17–6 in our favour. I dropped a goal and gave Tony O'Reilly a scoring pass, so I felt I had done enough to earn my keep.

On the return journey to Sydney for the second Test, we stopped at Tamworth to play a New South Wales Country XV. On the flight from Brisbane, we flew over miles and miles of absolutely nothing but Tamworth itself had a beautiful setting in the hills.

This should have been an easy game and indeed we won 27–14. However, by half time we were down to thirteen men. On another brick-hard pitch, both John Young and Bryn Meredith tore hamstrings and by the end of the game we were down to twelve men when Bill Mulcahy had to go off with an injured shoulder. Although they stayed on the pitch until the end of the game, Gordon Wood (father of future Ireland and Lions hooker,

Keith) had a broken finger and Stan Coughtrie had injured his back to such an extent that he didn't play again on tour. Add the already injured Niall Brophy, Mick English, Ray Prosser and Haydn Morgan to that list and the remaining party was looking decidedly thin.

Our overnight train journey back to Sydney and the Coogee Bay Hotel served to illustrate, again, the distances involved moving around Australia. Gordon Waddell was waiting for us at the hotel so that was one more, if jet-lagged, body to fill the gaps.

The same back division and front-row were retained for the second Test with enforced changes made in the second- and back-rows. We won 24–3 and I wrote in my diary, 'Very pleasant to record such a convincing win in the last game in Australia. The first half was a bit ragged with Bev doing some good kicking but generally there was very little combined play. They scored first with a penalty by Ken Donald, but we replied immediately. Bev broke right, passed to Malcolm who fed Peter and then took a return pass to score a good try, converted by David which gave us a narrow lead at half-time.

'The second half was completely ours with the forwards dominating all phases of the game – we were going forward all the time. Tony came in off his wing to make an extra man and Malcolm and Peter again exchanged passes for Malcolm to score. David again converted. We were right on top now and Bev scored a typical side-stepping try followed by Ronnie who got a try from a line-out at close range. Next, I made an extra man for Tony to drag his way over at the corner and I converted with my first kick in Australia. I also kicked a late penalty to finish the scoring.'

Australia had been great hosts and no pushovers in the Tests, but of course the centrepiece of the tour was New Zealand. And so it was that we readied ourselves for our flight across the

Tasman and our twenty-five match trek across the great spiritual home of rugby union.

EIGHT

LAND OF THE LONG WHITE CLOUD

If our passage through Australia was somewhat low key, our arrival in Auckland at 11 p.m. on a Sunday night changed all that. At the airport we were welcomed by the great and good of New Zealand rugby, backed by a large crowd of enthusiastic supporters.

After an overnight stop in Auckland, we flew on to Napier – the venue for our first game against Hawke's Bay. I wrote in my diary, 'The welcome to Napier can only be described as ROYAL and quite unbelievable. The streets were decorated with flags and lined by spectators for at least half a mile. It was a beautiful day and we were individually announced onto an open-air stage and entertained by Maori dancers.'

This turned out to be the norm rather than the exception as we toured the country. The two most noteworthy were the processions laid on on the morning of our games in Hamilton and New Plymouth.

There was much more build-up for our first game in New Zealand than there had been for even the Tests in Australia, and the game started with the ground packed to capacity with a

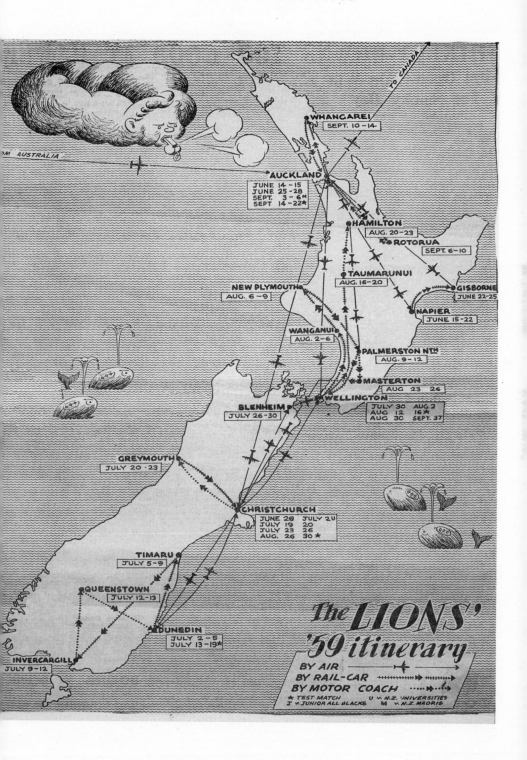

record crowd of 22,000. The level of enthusiasm in New Zealand was eye-opening for someone from Edinburgh. Everywhere you went you were a known figure. There were special supplements in the newspapers and photographs everywhere. The stands and terraces and pitch-sides were crammed everywhere we played. It was an extraordinary atmosphere to play in.

Vivian Jenkins wrote, 'The day and the playing surface were alike perfect and the Lions' backs gave a superb display. Hewitt scored four magnificent tries, one after a run of seventy yards, and Scotland, from full-back of all places, scored three more – in succession at that – an extraordinary performance for a so-called "last line of defence". He will soon be qualifying for a new description, seven-eighths or some such.' The final score of 52–12 was the highest number of points scored by any touring side in New Zealand, so we had laid down a marker.

Our third game in New Zealand, and ninth on tour, against Auckland, was expected to be one of our toughest games outwith the Tests. This prediction was well justified and we were happy to win narrowly 15–10 having been behind into the last quarter of an hour and then under a lot of pressure until the final whistle. It was a very forward-dominated game with little back play. Our forwards stood up well to the continuous pounding and lasted the pace better than Auckland but at no stage were we as effective in the loose. Having said that, I thought that Haydn Morgan at openside had an outstanding game. It was a good and most encouraging win in our hardest game so far.

As we flew to the South Island for the next eight matches, putting fifteen fit players onto the pitch had now become a serious problem. Three backs, Niall Brophy, Stan Coughtrie and Mick English would not play again on tour and the problems in the front-row were just as acute. Ronnie Dawson had played eight, and Hugh McLeod and Syd Millar had each played seven of the nine games so far – a really punishing workload. Andy

Mulligan had arrived to replace Stan Coughtrie – just in time – because he had to play four games in a row while Dickie Jeeps recovered from an injured shoulder.

In Christchurch, against a New Zealand Universities XV, Noel Murphy, who was a flanker, played on the wing, Hugh McLeod was moved from prop to hooker and with no appointed vice-captain, perhaps because we were playing against a team of students, I was given the captaincy. We built up a lead of 25 points but they responded with 13 points of their own which led overall to a most enjoyable game to play in. They were also very hospitable and for the first time on tour the two teams socialised well into the evening.

As a point of interest, although kicking with the instep is now the norm, it was a novelty in New Zealand in 1959. I kicked three goals with my instep against New Zealand Universities, which generated a lot of press comment and interest.

At school it was frowned upon to kick in this manner as it – apparently – smacked too much of football, but in the Edinburgh area at that time, although not common, it certainly could be very effective – as Royal High School contemporary, Jimmy Lacey, proved to our cost.

In New Zealand with the Lions, Terry Davies, John Faull, David Hewitt, Bev Risman and Malcolm Thomas were all regular orthodox place kickers for club and country, so to get any kicks at all I had to do something different. I ended up taking kicks from wide out on the left side of the pitch as the round-the-corner style widened the angle. It was not unusual for David Hewitt, Bev Risman and myself to be taking kicks during the same game.

With New Zealand using only Don Clarke, we put ourselves at a disadvantage by not concentrating on one kicker. Our most consistent kicker under pressure was Terry Davies so that policy would have meant fewer games for me.

Throughout my career I had spells kicking with my toe and with my instep and had some success with both but at best my place kicking could be described, rather like my current putting, as streaky.

Our next game in Dunedin, against Otago, had Hugh McLeod still hooking but with Haydn Morgan joining Noel Murphy, meaning two forwards in the three-quarter line. Malcolm Thomas was playing at stand-off (our fourth choice in the position) and I was kept as captain. As Otago had beaten the 1950 Lions we were left in no doubt that their present vintage expected to do a repeat performance. Throughout our time in New Zealand we had the reputation of good weather following us about. Not on this occasion, however, as the pitch was a bit of a mud bath. We managed to reach half-time in the lead but, against the elements in the second half, our makeshift back division rather lost the plot against a very savvy top provincial side and lost, by 26–8.

Our next Saturday fixture was in Invercargill against Southland. It just happened that Southland had also beaten the 1950 Lions and again we were left in no doubt that they were looking for history to repeat itself. Talk about going from the frying pan into the fire.

Ronnie Dawson was back as hooker, with Hugh McLeod back at prop, his tenth start in thirteen games. Bill Patterson, an uncapped Englishman, had joined us and was playing in the centre. Dickie Jeeps had recovered from injury and I became the fifth stand-off on tour.

The next stop on the journey south from Invercargill is the South Pole and on the day of the game we got weather to prove it. The conditions were awful, wet and windy, and made for ten-man rugby. On the day, we went even further and played nine-man rugby. The forwards never took a backwards step and Dickie kept putting the ball in front of them. When we got within striking range I tried to drop a goal. In the first half I had one success and in the second a rare one off my left foot.

I also hit the post with a third effort which rebounded nicely off a post for Peter Jackson to scoop up for a try. With the first Test in Dunedin due the following Saturday, we were more than pleased to come away with an 11–6 victory.

On the bus on the return journey to Dunedin we had an overnight stop at the then embryonic winter sports resort of Queenstown. We learned there that Niall Brophy and Mick English were to be sent home. Stan Coughtrie had already gone home at his own request. This caused unrest among the squad but with the management adamant that it was for everyone's benefit, the mini revolt came to nothing. Niall and Mick did have the last laugh, however, as they were sent home by sea and eventually arrived back in the UK after the rest of us.

With the first Test of a series generally considered to be the best opportunity for a win for the touring side – because of the advantage of having played several games together – the pressure was mounting. Our injury crisis had taken a turn for the better and the back division was the same as had played the two Tests in Australia. Not all the forwards were available, but the eight who played – Hugh McLeod, Ronnie Dawson, Gordon Wood, Rhys Williams, Roddy Evans, Ken Smith, John Faull and Noel Murphy – were close to being the first-choice selection.

This was an agonising game to lose. We scored four tries in a total of 17 points but were beaten by six penalty goals by Don Clarke for a total of 18 points. In my diary I wrote, 'A game which was dominated by the forwards but which lacked the spark associated with an international. Their scrum-half did a lot of high kicking back to his forwards but they were rarely well placed and Dickie dealt with most of them. They had a slight territorial edge in the first quarter and Don Clarke kicked two out of three penalty opportunities. The second quarter was ours and we fought back hard. David kicked a penalty and we scored two quick tries before half-time. Bev made a half opening, passed to Malcolm who sent in Tony unopposed. Bev again put in a low kick towards their line which bounced badly for the defence and Malcolm taking advantage scored. David and I, respectively, missed the conversions.

'The All Blacks staged quite an onslaught after half-time but we scored from our own twenty-five. They heeled from a scrum, Roger Urbahn broke and passed inside – fortunately for us to Roddy, who made it to the halfway line before passing to Ken who sent Peter away up the touchline to score at the corner. No-one had seen Peter run straight for so far before. Don Clarke then kicked another penalty to bring the score to 12–9 in our favour. They pressed hard for the equaliser but again we scored from our own twenty-five. They misdirected a pass and the ball went loose. Bev got a boot to it and just as it looked as though it would go into touch, it took an awkward bounce and this time Malcolm kicked it infield and into their half. I then gave the ball another hefty fly-hack, picked it up about five yards from the line, sold a dummy, then passed to Malcolm who scored wide out. Bev converted to make the score 17–9 in our favour with only twenty minutes to play. I thought we had made it, but it wasn't to be. Don kicked three more goals, ably abetted by the referee, and the less said about the last quarter of an hour the better. I have never been so disappointed or in such a bad temper at the end of a game before and for the first time ever I saw players crying in the dressing room.'

Until the last quarter of an hour, there seemed to be no criticism of the referee, but from full-back it is actually surprisingly difficult to have an opinion on his, or any others', many decisions. However, I am in no doubt that one of the final three penalties went over the top of a post. With no neutral touch judges in those days, Mick English, who thought as I did, kept his flag down to signal no goal but was overruled by the referee.

The final penalty was given for offside against Gordon Wood.

The New Zealand forwards were dribbling the ball, which hit Dickie Jeeps on the leg and rebounded to hit Gordon. He did not play the ball. The ball hit him so the decision should have been a scrum for accidental offside rather than a penalty.

These were both marginal decisions. Who knows what would have happened if the ball had hit an extension of the post and perhaps Gordon could have got out of the way? Together, however, they meant that for us the game ended on a sour note.

The New Zealanders were, as always, extremely focused and really hard to beat, but they played to a pretty limited game-plan. It was nine- and ten-man rugby. But, although they didn't do very much, what they did, they did with conviction and pace – so even if you knew what was coming, it was very hard to cope with. Apart from the performance of their pack during the third Test, I wouldn't say that they were anywhere near the best side I played against – they had some good players but their tactics were limited.

For the record, directly from the kick-off after their final penalty, our forwards drove the ball up to the line and Ken Smith is still adamant that he scored a legitimate try only to be pulled back for a previous infringement. On this occasion, I was definitely too far away to have an opinion but Ken is a very honourable man.

Hence my bad temper and tears in the dressing room.

'They really deserved to win the first Test, they played a lot better than us,' confessed Terry Lineen years later in the book, *Behind the Silver Fern: Playing Rugby for New Zealand*. 'The only real training run we had was on the Thursday because you couldn't have a hard run on the Friday. We were completely outplayed but we never liked to lose.'

The dinner that night was not our finest hour. We had one notorious roll-thrower in the party which would have been bad enough, but as we had started our meal with oysters, the missiles were a bit more dangerous. The top table was not amused and at the next team meeting we were told that a repeat performance would not be tolerated.

After a bus trip across the South Island for a mid-week game against West Coast–Buller in Greymouth (which we won 58–3), we were back in Christchurch for the fixture against Canterbury, always one of the top provincial teams. Our telephone calls home were strictly rationed, perhaps two or three only during the five months we were away. Doreen's twenty-first birthday coincided with the Canterbury game, so I had booked a call home. With the time differential, the first news of what had happened to the Lions in New Zealand reached the UK in time for a snippet on a Saturday morning radio breakfast programme. So on her twenty-first birthday, Doreen woke to the headlines, *Lions lose to Canterbury by 20 points to 14, Ken Scotland carried off on a stretcher.* Fortunately, with that precious phone call already booked, I was quickly able to report that there was no serious damage done. Almost fifty years later, Dennis Young, the Canterbury hooker recalled the incident. 'Ross Smith came off his wing and hit Scotland in a full-frontal collision. As he departed on a stretcher his face was the colour of chalk.' It was a fair tackle then, which I didn't see coming, but as no arms were used it would now be illegal. It was disappointing to lose another provincial game, but not too surprising as we played most of the second half with only thirteen men – Ken Smith had had to go off before me.

For our last midweek game in the South Island, we headed for its most northerly point in the wine-growing area of Marlborough. With no medical presence travelling with the team, I paid two visits to the local New Zealand Air Force station for treatment for my bruised ribs. It turned out that my injuries were fairly minor and I was able to play the following Saturday against Wellington.

Our first visit to the capital city was hectic socially, with a parliamentary reception, and official welcome speech from the Prime Minister, Walter Nash, on our first evening. The second evening, the day before our next game, we were hosted at a cocktail party by the New Zealand Rugby Union. I noted in my diary that in our three days in Wellington, we listened to eighteen speeches.

All but one of our remaining fourteen games in New Zealand would now be played in the North Island. With inter-island rivalry intense, and with the Lions having lost two provincial games in the south, it became a matter of pride to the locals that the same should be repeated in the north.

Considering all this off-field pressure, our 21–6 win over Wellington was particularly pleasing. It is a game that I remember well because it was quite unusual. The combination of forwards winning possession on the front foot and the half-backs using the ball so cleverly that we never put ourselves under pressure behind the gain line is a great formula to aim for but is seldom achieved. It suited me well to be little more than an admiring spectator and I soon forgot my bruised ribs.

We had three games to play before returning to Wellington for the second Test. Generally, the midweek games in the North Island were harder than in the South and also the geography was somehow more confusing. When we played against Taranaki in New Plymouth, I had been there for three days before I realised that we were by the seaside, although the name should have given me a hint.

Back in Wellington for the second Test, our injury problems, particularly in the backs, were acute. Of the seven possible stand-offs in the original party, only Malcolm Thomas and Malcolm Price were fit. Mick English had gone back to Ireland and Bev Risman, Gordon Waddell and David Hewitt were all injured. I'd picked up a fairly minor knee injury in the Tuesday game earlier in the week and also couldn't be considered. After much deliberation, Malcolm Thomas was picked in the centre with Malcolm Price becoming our sixth stand-off in sixteen games in New Zealand.

Playing with the wind in the first half, the All Blacks scored two unconverted tries to lead 6–0 at half-time. With the wind at our backs, we fought back to take the lead at 8–6 with quarter of an hour to go. Just as it looked as though we could square the series, they created space close to our line and, with men to spare, Don Clarke scored close to the posts for a converted try. In this instance there was no sense of injustice. It was a good game to watch and our depleted side competed courageously – but on balance, the better side won.

I think Don Clarke was underrated as a full-back. He had a reputation as a kicker, and as a lumbering player – but he tackled well, his positioning was excellent, and he had much more all-round ability than he was given credit for.

We won our next three games in the North Island before flying south for the crucial third Test in Christchurch. The toughest of these matches was against Waikato, home province of Don Clarke and his brother, Ian. The main feature was that Don missed all seven of his penalty attempts, showing a fallibility, which we had not seen before. Sufficiently recovered from my knee injury, I took my turn as touch judge and was able to enjoy our 14–0 victory.

For the third Test, Phil Horrocks-Taylor, who had recently arrived from the Cornish beaches as a replacement, became our seventh stand-off in New Zealand. I wrote in my diary: 'We went into the third Test with high hopes, but we were badly beaten. On paper, apart from Phil instead of Bev, I felt that we had selected our strongest side. The trouble was that, subconsciously, we went on to the field thinking that it must be our turn to have a bit of luck, but we did not work hard enough for a win. Our forwards were hammered and as a result the backs never had any room to move the ball. Their pack was the best I have ever played against and we were really up against it. We had no room to pass the ball at all and some of our tactical kicking was bad – Ralph Caulton had a field day off our kicks. Don Clarke played well and kicked a lovely left-foot drop goal. There seems to be a lot to be said for their defensive set up round the scrums. Both flankers go for the scrum-half with the stand-off lying flat and with the scrum-half doing any defensive kicking. Roger Urbahn seemed to have much more time than Dickie. It was a perfect day for open rugby and I am sure we were stronger in the backs but we were unable to use that advantage because of a complete lack of second phase possession.'

The final score of 22 (including four tries) to 8 (one try) was proof of their superiority. If I was hard on our forwards it was only because I was so impressed by the All Black eight. On a firm ground and with a dry ball they were relentless in both attack and defence. Not all their names are well known, but some are legendary – Whineray, Hemi, Irwin, MacEwan, Hill, Meads, Conway and Tremain.

With the Test series now lost, it should have been a subdued group who flew back to the North Island for the final five games in New Zealand. Although it was not a private flight, Tony O'Reilly and Andy Mulligan managed to commandeer the in-flight loudspeaker system and raised morale with very clever take-offs of our management, the New Zealand management and members of the International Board who happened to be on board. They were also merciless in cutting their teammates down to size.

Both scrum-halves were now injured and for the next two games I got the short straw. In the first game against the New Zealand Juniors, Gordon Waddell was the unlucky stand-off and he was not at all happy with the service he was getting. A season later, arriving at Melrose to play in the sevens for Cambridge

University with two stand-offs and no scrum-half, Gordon point blank refused to play if I intended to reprise the role of scrum-half. He played the position so effectively that we won the tournament, but that is another story. In my defence, Gordon scored three tries against the Juniors in our 29–9 win, so he must have got some decent possession.

My second game at scrum-half was against the New Zealand Maoris and running on to the pitch in Auckland, I had never felt so terrified in my life. It was blazing hot, the ground was brick-hard and the rattle of studs as the teams ran on to the pitch sounded like a preview of what would be happening on my back after every line-out. It was the only game on tour that we did not score a try – and my service to Phil Horrocks-Taylor was no doubt part of the problem – but it was, in general, an unpleasant game of rugby with boots and fists flying right from the start. The forwards gave me great protection at the lines-out, with Ray Prosser handing me ball on a plate. On the day, I found putting the ball into the scrum the most stressful of my duties. Getting our put-in to the scrums at the right time, at the right pace and landing on the exact spot to Bryn Meredith's satisfaction was nerve-racking. Three penalties from Terry Davies and a drop goal by David Hewitt were enough to preserve our North Island winning record, out-with the Tests.

I have only recently been shown a picture of me 'scoring a try' in the game, which was disallowed by the referee (see the picture section). Previously I had seen a picture just after the referee had made his decision and I am staring at him in disbelief with my arms aloft. It would certainly have resulted at a practice game at school in my being sent off for so obviously questioning the referee's decision. At the end of a longish dribble I picked up the ball just as I fell over the line to score what I thought was a perfectly legitimate try – but the referee called for a knock-on. You can probably understand my frustration.

Having played in the last four games, I was surprised to be picked at full-back for the last mid-week game at Rotorua against Thames Valley–Bay of Plenty. Perhaps I should not have been because at this stage of the tour Terry was putting in some very good performances, not least with his place kicking, and looked set to play full-back in the fourth Test. We got off to a good start, despite Jeff Butterfield only lasting about ten minutes, and shortly before half-time we were leading 21–0. The home side then did what no other opponents had done – they ran at us with ball in hand, and by half-time had reduced the deficit by 11 points. The locals were now inspired and backed by a noisy boisterous crowd they took the lead at 24–21 with time running out.

Vivian Jenkins later wrote, 'With defeat staring them in the face, the Lions did at last arouse themselves and the game was like a Test match from then to the finish. Even so, it needed one of Scotland's very best efforts in the dying moments to pluck the brand from the burning. Now in the centre – for Malcolm Thomas, injured, had gone to full-back – he regained possession after a movement initiated by himself had broken down, and raced through a gap between vainly clutching hands to score close to the posts. It was a life-safer. With the referee looking at his watch Malcolm Thomas's conversion just carried the Lions home.'

The ultimate accolade for me, however, came from Hugh McLeod, who gave me a huge hug as we left the pitch and said, 'Scotland, you wee bugger, that's just what you did to Hawick at Goldenacre last September.' Such praise is praise indeed.

Rotorua is noted for its thermal springs, and strong smell of sulphur, and one of the highlights after the game was to go to a Maori family party and end up having a hot bath at the foot of the garden.

From Rotorua, we had a nine-hour railcar journey to Whangarei, the most northerly point on our journey round New

Zealand. Despite the fact that this was our twenty-fourth game in New Zealand and we had lost the Test series, our welcome was undiminished. This was the last opportunity for a provincial side to beat us on the North Island and the locals and their supporters were up for the clash. The goalposts were claimed to be the tallest in the world at eighty-four feet at one end and seventy-six at the other. Don Clarke himself would have had difficulty putting one over the top.

For this game, I was selected to start in the centre, not my favourite position. With only the fourth and final Test to come, our 35–13 win over a team who definitely thought they could intimidate us was a big boost to morale. The forwards were all superb and Bev, despite taking a nasty punch on the face early on, made a very good comeback. My opposite number in the centre spent the whole game obstructing me, with or without the ball. I had the last laugh, however, scoring two poacher's tries from lucky bounces of the ball. Terry had a dream game at full-back and his place-kicking was well-nigh perfect.

The final Test in Auckland attracted a record crowd in New Zealand of 63,000 spectators. Terry Davies was selected at full-back, but I was thrilled to still make it into the team in the centre. The weather couldn't have been worse, there had been thunderstorms and rain all night, and they had played a couple of warm-up games on the pitch so it was a bit of a quagmire. I wrote in my diary, 'A tremendous climax to a most enjoyable but very strenuous tour. The ground was generally soft and slippery with a sea of mud in the centre of the field. They put in the early pressure and Don succeeded with his third penalty attempt after ten minutes. From a scrum just inside our own half, on the left side of the pitch, Tony came off his wing, took the ball outside Bev, made a break, threw an overhead pass to me, I drew Don and sent Peter off on a tortuous run to the corner. There was no further scoring before half-time. The second half was better than the first and as time wore on we became more and more on top. We took the lead when Andy went blind from a scrum and put Tony in at the corner. Shortly afterwards Don kicked the equaliser and the game was really alive and full of movement. We put in ten minutes of pressure at the end of which Bev scored a lovely try. From a scrum on the left-hand side of the field, Andy broke open, reverse-passed to Bev who flashed past the remnants of their pack, sidestepped McPhail and beat Don on a straight run to the corner.

'It was a good international played in adverse conditions and I have never been so delighted to win a game. If ever a captain deserved to lead a team to victory it was Ronnie, because throughout the whole tour he had shown a perfect example both on and off the field. The only possible criticism was that he was too conscientious for his own good. The forwards lasted the pace well with Haydn outstanding in the loose and Rhys and Ray in the lines-out, but they all worked like two men. Andy played courageously and well and Bev showed what a great football brain he has – for him it was a tremendous comeback, having spent time with his leg in plaster. Tony and Peter took their chances well and David and I had an inconspicuous day in the centre, except for my first three left-footed tactical kicks, which were so bad as to be horribly noticeable. Terry gave one of the best exhibitions of full-back play I have ever seen and I doubt if I would have played in as many Tests had Terry been fit the whole time. The New Zealand team, and public, took the defeat well and the Test series itself was played in an excellent spirit throughout.'

Nearly sixty years on what do I recall from the final Test? I discovered to my cost that tactical kicking from inside centre is quite different from stand-off. As I was never called upon to make a tackle, I realised the All Blacks played to a strict and limited tactical plan. I'm not complaining, but in their shoes

I should have been targeted as a weakness. Towards the end of the game, Don Clarke had an opportunity to kick an equalising penalty. The ball flew across the face of the posts and was fielded by Peter Jackson in our in-goal area. I was next to Peter and I could see him eyeing the possibility of setting off upfield to try and score a try at the other end. I remember shouting at him to touch the ball down and finish the game and I was preparing to make my first tackle of the game to stop him. It was no time for heroics. Luckily, he saw sense and touched the ball down.

'The blast of the whistle is long, definite, final,' wrote Terry McLean in his book on the tour, *Kings of Rugby*. 'The game is over. And the Lions leap in the air in utter joy. They have won. What is more, they have reached the resting place in which, forever, they will inspire respect, admiration and even adulation.'

I will always remember the contrast in the dressing from that of the first Test. Utter despair turned to an elation, tinged with a little relief, that we had finally regained some pride by somehow managing to find the communal will and strength of character to produce that performance in the thirty-first game on tour. For everyone playing, and in the stand, as well, we took a lot out of that. It was the first time the Lions had won a Test in New Zealand since 1930. And, with that, Hugh McLeod and I became the first Scots ever to win a Test match against the All Blacks. Not many Scots have added to that number since: Ian McLauchlan, Gordon Brown, Andy Irvine, Ian McGeechan and Gavin Hastings.

In over three months in New Zealand we travelled the length and breadth of the North and South Islands, Whangarei to Invercargill, and Greymouth to Gisborne. Everywhere we played, and at stops we made on our travels in between, we were met by enthusiastic crowds. Flying over an active volcano, Lake Taupo, in the North Island and spending a night in Queenstown, in the South were examples of the breath-taking scenic beauty we enjoyed in the country.

If bedrooms with en suite facilities were uncommon and menus fairly predictable as we moved from one hotel to another, the friendliness of all the local people we met more than compensated.

The feeling that we were a long way from home and that everyone was rooting for the opposition created in us a bit of a laager mentality. A regret I have is that because we were self-sufficient as a group, I spent less time than I should getting to know the opposition players.

On the way home, we completed a circumnavigation of the globe with stops in Fiji, Honolulu, San Francisco, Seattle, Vancouver, Toronto, New York, London and Glasgow before reaching Edinburgh 144 days after leaving. En route, we won two games in Canada. In Vancouver we were given a really tough game by a largely Canadian-born team, while in Toronto we were much too strong for a team composed of mainly ex-pat Brits.

By the most important judgement, losing the Test series to New Zealand 3–1, the 1959 tour was a failure. By most other criteria it was a huge success. Two Test wins in Australia got us off to an encouraging start, but it in no way prepared us for the intensity of the way rugby was played and regarded in New Zealand. There was no anonymity anywhere. I compared it at the time to a Hearts player walking in Gorgie Road or a Hibs player walking down Easter Road. It was a bit like being a public exhibit. Whenever possible we played to our acknowledged tactical plan, which was to use the pace in our backs and which was also good to watch. We attracted full houses everywhere we played and overall we averaged five tries per game. The 582 points we scored in New Zealand was a record for any touring side in that country.

'That was a great series in 1959 and they were a good side,' said Wilson Whineray in *Behind the Silver Fern*:. 'I think overall they were one of the best sides I ever played. Had they the forward power of later Lions teams they would have donkeyed us, to be honest. The backline was the finest I've played against. We were very lucky to get out with a 3–1 victory, 2–2 would have been a better reflection.'

'They were a good team to play against,' reflected Colin Meads in *Behind the Silver Fern*. 'They had brilliant backs. That 1959 backline was as good as any we've had tour this country. People used to say if they got forty per cent of the ball we'd get beaten.'

While the backs, as usual, were taking most of the kudos, the forwards were nothing short of heroic. For only fifteen forwards to battle through thirty-three games of highly physical rugby speaks volumes. Whereas the softies in the backs had three replacements joining the tour, the forwards just had to get on with it. It is invidious to pick out individuals, but Ronnie Dawson for his leadership, Rhys Williams for his overall strength and know-how and Hugh McLeod for his durability and ever presence were outstanding. Hugh was a fantastic tourist. He had been to South Africa in 1955 and hadn't made the Test team, but in 1959 he was one of our anchor men. He didn't drink, he was first up for breakfast, he was first on the bus, he was first to every scrum and every line-out, and did everything he was ever asked to do. He was just a perfect guy to have on tour – I have always had a huge regard for him. He was an incredibly strong and clever rugby player.

He was pretty popular in a dour sort of way. He was called 'the Abbot', of course, referring to his monastic lifestyle. But he was by no means unique as a teetotaller – I would think six or seven of the guys in the squad were non-drinkers. To be honest, it wasn't a hugely boozy tour at all.

Because there were only five back rows chosen, David Marques several times played out of position at No. 8 and never made a backward step. This in turn put pressure on the second row where both Roddy Evans and Bill Mulcahy rose magnificently to the challenge. The back row, being a man short right from the start as it were, were all in at the thick end. Alan Ashcroft, John Faull, Haydn Morgan, Ken Smith and Noel Murphy were all big aggressive forwards equally at home in attack or defence and their contribution in the tight and loose was immense. The other three props, Gordon Wood, Syd Millar and Ray Prosser were consistently solid in the scrums and providing support at the lines-out. Bryn Meredith was in the unfortunate position of playing in the same position as the captain and that curtailed the number of games he played. When he did play he was very effective and a good leader of the forwards. If he ever complained about not being selected for a Test, as was suggested in the press at the time, he must have spoken in Welsh for I never caught as much as a whisper. Throughout the tour he was the epitome of the good team man. So much for the forwards – I thought they were all absolutely outstanding.

None of the above, however, lessens the fact that at times the backs could have done with more second phase possession on the front foot. To meet our stated objective of playing open fifteen-man running rugby, each game had to be taken in context. The weather conditions, the state of the pitch and who happened to be playing stand-off all had a bearing on the way the game was played but the quantity and especially the quality of the possession provided by the forwards was the essential consistent requirement.

Of the backs, three of the original choices, Niall Brophy, Stan Coughtrie and Mick English had no opportunity to make an impression on the pitch. They were all humorous characters in their own way and Mick entertained us with an extensive repertoire of Irish rebel songs and we were sorry to see them go. Of the replacements, Andy Mulligan was there longest and made the most impact, culminating in creating the opportunity for two of our tries in the fourth Test. Although they both played in a Test against New Zealand, and played well in difficult circumstances, neither Bill Patterson nor Phil Horrocks-Taylor played enough to challenge for a place when everyone was fit. Jeff Butterfield, who had been one of the Lions' stars in South Africa in 1955, suffered injury after injury and must have been bitterly disappointed to play in so few games and to be unable to do himself justice. Despite that, he was a perfect tourist, showing an outstanding example off the pitch especially to the younger players. Malcolm Thomas, our survivor from the 1950 tour, turned out to be a real workhorse in 1959. Although he had lost a bit of pace, he was still extremely skilful and tactically aware and whether playing at stand-off, centre, wing or full-back, as he did on tour, he never looked out of place.

Gordon Waddell, one of my closest friends at Cambridge, was never quite able to do himself justice because of a series of knee injuries. He returned home early to have a knee operation in the hope of a quick return to action in the new season that was now underway at home. Of the three remaining wingers after Niall Brophy went home, John Young, partly because of injuries, played the fewest games. He was the quickest of the three and scored a good try in the second Test in New Zealand, but was always behind Peter Jackson and Tony O'Reilly in the pecking order. Peter was neither particularly fast nor well built by international rugby standards, but he was very elusive and deceptively difficult to tackle. In total he scored nineteen tries. Tony, on the other hand, was both fast and strong, and given just a hint of a chance he loved scoring tries. The seventeen which he scored in New Zealand, out of a total of twenty-one on tour, was a record for any tourist in that country.

At the tender age of nineteen, David Hewitt was our number one centre three-quarter. His most obvious asset was electric pace, but for his age he also had an impressive all-round maturity and had a great temperament for the big occasion. Malcolm Price was number two centre. In a back division which received lots of plaudits for its pace and skill, Malcolm played his full part. I think he was largely underrated in the press – but not by his teammates.

Of all the injuries we suffered in New Zealand, the most damaging was Bev Risman's broken leg. Out for over a month he missed eight games including the second and third Tests in New Zealand. Taking a line through his outstanding performances in the first and fourth Tests, it is not stretching credibility too far to suggest that we would have won the second Test had he been fit and that overall the series would have been drawn. History cannot be rewritten, but Bev was comfortably our best stand-off tactically and, in attack and defence, he brought out the best in the players around about him.

Dickie Jeeps had a very good tour. I enjoyed playing with him. He was courageous in fielding, on the retreat, most of the many box kicks put over his head and thereby saving me a lot of physical punishment. Dickie was very good at knowing when to give his stand-off the ball, but most of all he enjoyed the unglamorous chores of working as a ninth forward in defence. Not as physically robust as Dickie, Andy Mulligan also played consistently well having a hand in all three tries we scored in winning the fourth Test.

I went on tour as number two full-back and came back in the same position. In Australia, Terry Davies' misfortune with injuries opened up opportunities for me, but by the end of the tour he was back to his very best. His performance in the fourth Test, and the week before against North Auckland, was a master-class of full-back play. I was very lucky with injuries and was only unavailable for selection for four out of the thirty-three games.

As an exercise in male bonding, a five-month rugby tour which takes you right round the world must take some beating. Throw in the fact that we changed roommates at each of our thirty-seven moves, we got to know each other very well. It was very much the highlight of my sporting career and the memories both on and off the field are as vivid as ever. As a group we have had three very successful reunions over the past fifty years and the mutual friendship and respect lives on. That was the big thing about touring, everybody became a personal friend. To meet some of those guys almost fifty years later might seem strange to outsiders but for us it is like we have never been away.

In 1960, *The Rugby Almanack of New Zealand* named a list of 'Five Players of the Year' from first-class matches in 1959, and I was flattered to be included. They carried the following profile:

Kenneth James Forbes Scotland (Cambridge University and Scotland) was one of the keenest and most popular of the British Isles team. Seemingly he was so keen to play whenever possible that he did not mind being given any position to fill. Most versatile, eager and lively, Scotland proved a most useful man to his team. He filled the last line of defence more often than not, and there showed how dangerous a clever fast-running full-back can be. He also played at centre-three-quarter, at stand-off half, and at scrum-half, and whilst not the perfect player in each position, was at least competent, and of considerable service.

Of but slender build, and weighing only 11st. 2lb., Scotland yet never shirked the centre of the struggle or evaded a tackle. His considerable value as a potential match-winner with his speed, elusiveness and eagerness to attack, was proved in a number of matches. His two dropped goals when at stand-off half against Southland were decisive factors in the Lions' victory; his great left-foot drop kick against Canterbury; another against Taranaki; three successive tries at the commencement of the second spell in the opening match against Hawke's Bay – when he was full-back; two fine tries when he played so effectively at centre against North Auckland; and that final match-winning try at Rotorua, when again playing at centre. Scotland perforce had to be full-back in the first and third Tests in the absence of Davies, but it was impossible to exclude such a valuable player from the last Test so he was placed at centre on that occasion. In his sixteen matches in this country he contributed 45 points, comprised of seven tries, three conversions, two penalty goals and four dropped goals.

He also played in four matches in Australia, being full-back on both Tests, and he totalled 17 points there with three tries, one conversion, one penalty goal and one dropped goal.

NINE

BACK TO BASICS

After all the long months of travel and adventure with the Lions, I arrived back in Edinburgh on Thursday 1 October with the advice of Alf Wilson, our manager – 'Take a decent break, you have been playing rugby for the best part of a year' – ringing in my ears. Stupidly, I could not resist the opportunity to play for Heriot's against Jedforest at Goldenacre on the Saturday and I picked up a niggling injury to my right ankle which took most of the rest of the season to heal completely.

In mid-October an England/Wales v Ireland/Scotland game at Twickenham provided a quick reunion for the Lions. In particular, it was an opportunity for me to show off Doreen and to meet Ann (to become Risman) and Pauline (to become Young). The game was won by England/Wales but naturally it was full of friendly rivalry. Playing with a heavily strapped ankle, the only thing I really remember was enjoying making a try-saving tackle on John Young in full flight.

Back at Cambridge, I was now secretary (effectively vice-captain) of the rugby club and I became much more aware of how the club was organised. The captain, with advice from the secretary and an assistant secretary (also a player), was in total charge of all playing decisions. This included the selection of two teams, training arrangements and all tactical decisions. Non-playing matters, like finance and fixtures, were looked after by a senior committee. Brothers Tom and Mike Hayward were, amongst other duties, groundsmen at Grange Road, our home pitch, and they were also responsible for all our kit and travel arrangements. At this point in the history of the rugby club, there was no shortage of money. How true it was I am not sure, but it was generally believed then that the income from the annual match against Oxford at Twickenham heavily subsidised all sports at both universities.

More importantly, I was aware that I would have to work hard to prepare for my final degree exams. For each of the five papers I was due to sit I had a supervisor whom I met, with one or two other students, on a regular basis. Our supervisor set us a topic and for our next visit we had to present an essay for his criticism and general discussion. This set a pattern of lectures or library in the morning, rugby in the afternoon and library again in the evening. As the weeks passed, I spent less and less time at lectures and more time researching topics in an array of libraries. The first port of call was the 'Seeley', the History faculty library, but to get the vital text book it was sometimes necessary to go to the university library or the magnificent Wren Library close to home at Trinity.

After an enforced four-week break, and with Gordon Waddell still recovering from a knee operation, I played stand-off in the last five games leading up to the Varsity match at Twickenham. We managed good wins against Leicester, Harlequins and Steele-Bodgers XV, but Oxford were deserved winners in the all-important one at Twickenham. The result, their three penalties to our one, summed up a rather disappointing game. With all the effort which goes in over the preceding eight weeks, it is always a bad game to lose but even worse knowing that we had failed to play even close to our potential. With six of the pack who had dominated the game the previous year outplayed on this occasion, and with the backs unable to supply any inspiration, it was a chastened group who attended the dinner at night. The dinner was quite unusual in that it was only attended by the thirty players, plus the two touch judges, who were the previous year's captains. Oxford celebrated and we put on our 'good losers' faces.

*

The 1960 Five Nations was not a successful one for Scotland. At Murrayfield France had a thirteen-point lead before we made any impression on the game. By the final whistle, we had fought back with a lot of spirit to reduce the margin to two points but at no time did we look like winning.

In Cardiff, we lost 8–0. My diary entry of 'a very poor display with no passion in the side' was echoed in all the press reports. Before our next game in Dublin, the papers were all calling for multiple changes.

With TV coverage of international rugby still very much in its infancy there was a much wider exposure and column inches in a range of newspapers than there is today. In the central belt alone, rugby correspondents for the *Scotsman*, *Glasgow Herald*, *Daily Express*, *Daily Mail*, *Bulletin*, *Edinburgh Evening News* and *Edinburgh Evening Dispatch* all felt free to select their XV for the next game. Naturally the *Glasgow Herald* picked more players from the west, but with rugby writers in the east known to have close connections with Edinburgh Academicals, Watsonians, Heriot's FP and Stewart's FP there were always some very skewed selections.

The official selectors limited their changes to six for the trip to Dublin. At a team meeting on the day before the game, Alf

Wilson, the chairman of selectors, while welcoming four new caps, gave the established players a verbal slaying for their performance in Cardiff.

It seemed to do the trick as we edged the result with a narrow 6–5 win. Despite the low scoring, the game was all action – as our games with Ireland usually were – and really enjoyable to play in. The return of captain and stand-off Gordon Waddell, with new scrum-half Brian Shillinglaw from Gala showing lots of promise, brought a sense of direction to the team. The injection of spirit and passion into the forwards came from Heriot's openside, David Edwards. Being asked to lead the forwards on his first cap was a huge responsibility but he rose to the task as to the manner born.

Encouraged by the win, an unchanged side was chosen to play England at Murrayfield. After twenty minutes we were sixteen points adrift without having played particularly badly, although I had a kick charged down which gifted them a converted try. The spirit, however, did continue from the Irish game and we managed to score twelve points before finally losing 21–12. It was the highest number of points scored in any of the games I played in the Five Nations. It was a really enjoyable game to play in and I append some anonymous press comments: 'It was one of the most exciting internationals seen at the ground and there was no disgrace in Scotland's defeat.' 'Scotland fully lived up to their new reputation gained in Dublin and the forwards made a magnificent fight of it.' 'It was a day for rejoicing that this great game can be played at such pace in such spirit at International level.'

At the start of term in January, I had been elected captain of the university XV which meant that up until the England game at the end of March, I was heavily involved in rugby at the expense of time I should have spent studying. To compensate, I used the peace and quiet of the National Library in Edinburgh during the Easter vacation to do some much-needed revision.

A pleasant, and eagerly anticipated, diversion from work was a visit to the Melrose Sevens with Cambridge University, who were the invited guest team that year. Our team selection was complicated by the fact that a combined Oxford/Cambridge short tour to America was due to coincide with Melrose. Because of work pressure, I was not going on the America trip but I had been partly involved in its organisation. The travel costs were to be funded by a wealthy young heiress who, along with her parents, had visited both Oxford and Cambridge. With the benefit of hindsight, it sounded much too good to be true and the team had assembled at Heathrow before the whole episode turned out to be a hoax.

However, it did mean that at the last minute we were able to assemble a stronger seven than we had anticipated doing. The problem of having two stand-offs and no scrum-half was solved unilaterally by Gordon Waddell refusing to play if he had to suffer me again at scrum-half, as he had done on the Lions tour against New Zealand Juniors. It was the right decision as he had a really good tournament playing at scrum-half.

The draw had done us no favours as we faced Hawick in the first round. Having won the previous week at Gala, and with the hugely experienced forward trio of Jack Hegarty, Hugh McLeod and Adam Robson (all Scottish internationalists), Hawick were overwhelming favourites. On our side, none of the forwards – Cameron Boyle, Mike Wetson and John Brash – had ever previously played in a Borders sevens tournament (Cameron and John were subsequently capped for Scotland), but it was their speed and youthful enthusiasm about the pitch which eventually enabled us to scrape through.

A relatively straightforward win against Stewart's FP in the second round set up a semi-final tie against the tournament hosts. Every time Melrose take the field at the Greenyards there is a palpable increase in tension and excitement. It is understandable that with all the history surrounding the birth of seven-a-side rugby in the town, the players' ambition to be in a winning team is always evident and hard to play against. With half-backs David Chisholm and Alec Hastie, and a youthful Jim Telfer in their seven, it took a classic scrum-half try from Gordon Waddell at the end of a very close tie to edge us into the final.

Had I been writing the script, I could have contrived nothing better than to play against Heriot's in the final. Four of the team I had played with when Heriot's won in 1957 and 1958 were now going to be in the opposition and I was to be directly marked by my young brother, Ronnie. For my father and sister, Elsie, having a family interest in seven out of the fifteen ties would have stopped the afternoon from dragging, but the final must have been nerve-wracking. The final score of 28–9 in Cambridge's favour was not a fair reflection on the run of play. The try score of 6–3 did more justice to Heriot's.

By chance, in the four ties we had beaten the four most successful sevens of the 1950s. In the introduction to his book, *The Official History of the Melrose Sevens*, Walter Allan wrote: 'The Cambridge University side of 1960 were regarded by some as the best team to have played at Melrose. With five Scotsmen in their ranks they were certainly one of the most popular.'

With possession being nine/tenths of the law in sevens, it was a triumph for our inexperienced forward trio.

It was appropriate, too, that Doreen who had been one of our few supporters in the crowd, took possession of the Ladies Cup and made sure that it stayed undamaged on its journey up the A7 to Edinburgh.

*

Returning to Cambridge after the Easter holidays, I now had just six weeks before I sat my final degree exams. I still had supervisions to attend and prepare for, but most of my time was now concentrated on revising topics I had previously covered. The fact that I had prepared for and written essays on these topics made revision easier. It did mean, however, that I was becoming more knowledgeable on a reduced range of topics, which meant that to some extent at least I needed the right questions to appear on the exam papers. The pattern that developed over the six weeks was to work all day ending up for a nightcap at the Mill. And even if I didn't manage to work *all* day, I did usually end up at the Mill.

On the first Saturday back, I went to Beckenham to play for London Scottish in a qualifying competition to reach the finals day of the Middlesex Sevens. By beating London Irish in the final we qualified to play at Twickenham the following Saturday. The same team (Rob Galbraith, replaced in the final by Ian Reid, Jim Shackleton, myself, Iain Laughland, Robin Marshall, captain, David Hayburn and Don Trow) won again, this time beating London Welsh in the final.

Apart from work, being president of the Trinity Field Club meant that I was invited to a commemoration feast (normally only for Dons and Scholars) and was included in a line-up to meet Queen Elizabeth, the Queen Mother, on the occasion of the opening of a new set of rooms. I was also, ex officio, included in a panel to judge a poetry writing competition, which was certainly a first for me.

The highlight of a limited cricket term was raising a Crusaders XI comprising only of Blues in other sports. I enjoyed keeping wicket to the opening pair of a javelin thrower and a wing-three-quarter with at first change a light-weight boxer.

By the time exam week arrived I was as well prepared as I was ever likely to be. The advice I had been given was to write as much as I possibly could, even if I had to tweak the question a little, and that the examiners liked the use of quotations. So I went in to the exams primed with a list of quotations to be used at all costs. What the examiner of my Anglo-Irish 1916-21 paper made of the quotation by Anthony Joseph Francis O'Reilly will never be known.

My holiday job in the investment department of the Scottish Widows was well under way when the results arrived. It was a relief just to have passed and I was very pleased, and a little surprised, to get a 2:2 honours degree.

That should have been the end of my time at university. To constitute a term at Cambridge there was an ancient rule that fifty breakfasts had to be taken in college. Also, to be awarded a degree, nine terms had to be spent in residence. While I qualified on the breakfasts, by missing a term being away with the Lions, I still had one term to do.

With exams now out of the way and with the rest of the summer in Edinburgh, I was now in a position to make plans with Doreen to achieve my third ambition. My first priority was to find a job, but whatever lay ahead we decided that we would be married the following Easter.

The experience of working in investments had been enjoyable but not fulfilling enough for me to consider it as a career.

Back in Cambridge for my last term, I discovered that as well as planning to beat Oxford in December and finding a job, I was expected to do some studying. My first suggestion that I do a term of Scottish history was ruled out on the basis that there was no-one in college who could act as my supervisor. I eventually settled for a course of industrial sociology, which was interesting and, as it happened, when I finally started work it turned out to be marginally relevant.

With the game against Oxford only eight weeks away, the selection committee of Mike Wade, Mike Wetson and myself already had a very good idea who would form the nucleus of the team. During the term we lost away to Cardiff and at home to

South Africa, but we also had good wins against Northampton and Leicester so we were in good shape for Twickenham. However, we had acquired a really difficult selection problem at prop forward where we were picking from strength. Two mature freshmen from Leeds University on a one-year course, Bev Dovey and David Wrench, had arrived to challenge the established pair Calum Bannerman and Cameron Boyle. Mike Wetson who was our hooker, was in the best position to judge but, like both Mike Wade and myself, was a close friend of both Calum and Cam. To make it even more personal, I had known Calum and Cam since playing against them in Heriot's against Merchiston school fixtures.

After much agonising, Bev and David got their Blues and Calum and Cam did not. Would any alternative selection have changed the result against Oxford? I think not.

Bev and David were both subsequently selected to play for England and Cam for Scotland. Calum was the one who missed out and I know that it meant a great deal to him. I like to think that we are still friends, but I do feel for him nearly sixty years after the event.

During the term, I was offered a teaching job at an English public school. With married accommodation being part of the package, this had an instant appeal. I had been very lucky with many of my teachers at school but I had also been aware of some who were just going through the motions. I still think that teaching is an admirable profession when done well but as I felt no vocation for the work to accept would have been for all the wrong reasons.

I went to London for career advice from Dan Drysdale, first in the line of – then five, now eight – Heriot's full-backs to be capped by Scotland. Since moving to London, he had built a successful business career in the timber industry. His advice was fatherly rather than specific but I appreciated his taking the time to meet me.

I had an unsuccessful interview in Corby for a position in a steel manufacturing company before accepting work as a trainee management consultant with Weston, Evans and Company based in Leicester. The owners had absolutely no connection with the local rugby club, but I did happen to be following in the footsteps of Bob McEwan, Tony O'Reilly and Phil Horrocks-Taylor.

With selection made and with a job organised, I could look forward to the game at Twickenham. Having experienced the highs and lows of winning and losing the only game that really counted in our season, I had the added incentive of wanting to appear in the record books as a winning captain.

On the day, our forwards, skilfully supported by Gordon Waddell and Trevor Wintle at half-back, were outstanding and we were 13–0 up at half-time. With the result being paramount, we played risk-free rugby in a rather dull second half which saw no change on the scoreboard.

Coming into the three-quarter line outside the outside centre I had a hand in one of the tries. Normally I liked to hold a line, draw the opposition full-back and put our winger in at the corner, but on this occasion I was being forced too wide, so I went on the outside and slipped a reverse pass to Alan Godson who cut behind the defence to score. At the time it probably looked a bit off the cuff, but it was a move that Alan and I had practised at Catterick four seasons previously but had never used or discussed since.

As a postscript to the three Varsity Matches I played in, our winning teams in 1958 and 1960 both had ten past, present or future internationalists, while our losing side in 1959 could only boast seven, plus one future England cricket captain in Tony Lewis.

At the ball after the game, I took great pleasure in introducing Doreen as my fiancée and showing off her engagement ring.

*

The last three weeks of December were hectic from a rugby point of view. In the fortnight between the two Scottish trials I played for Cambridge in Dublin against Dublin Wanderers, a Scottish XV against the Combined Services and for Heriot's against Melville College. On Boxing Day, I played for London Scottish against Edinburgh Accies in Edinburgh and the following day for the Barbarians against Leicester in Leicester.

The trip to Leicester was useful in as much as I managed to organise digs on London Road for my start of work there in less than a week's time.

My first training assignment was in a local shoe factory. Increasing productivity in both manpower and in the use of capital was the holy grail of the manufacturing industry in the UK at that time. Under the influence of Sir Charles Clore, who consolidated many of the well-known brand names into the British Shoe Corporation, the shoe industry was rapidly changing from a fashion base to a mass production philosophy.

During the six weeks I spent in Leicester, my first in the 'real world', rugby continued to dominate. I realised that I could no longer play any midweek games, but after only three days of finding my way around the shop floor I was off to Paris for the first game in the 1961 Five Nations. On three of the next five Saturdays, I went to London to play for London Scottish and the other two were Tests in Edinburgh against South Africa and Wales.

We won the Welsh game, rather unspectacularly, 3–0, but I was pleased to have set up Arthur Smith for the crucial try that won the game. 'Intuitive genius,' *The Scotsman*'s Jack Dunn called it – 'a peach of a pass.' I was also able to contribute to the defensive side of the game when putting in a tackle on the flying Dewi Webb, which helped save a try. 'Down the wing he went like a bullet,' wrote Dunn. 'But hey presto, and to the profound relief of Scots patriots, KJF Scotland, who had played immaculately, got across and brought him down on the corner flag.' The crowd for that game was 70,000, a post-war record for Murrayfield, and although the scoring was as low as it's possible to get, they still celebrated like mad when it was over.

On the Monday after the Wales game, I started my first proper assignment, under supervision, in a shoe factory in Banbridge, County Down. Weston Evans had evolved a system for the shoe industry called focal point planning, which was an early version of critical path analysis. In very simple terms, it involved identifying bottlenecks in the production process and then finding solutions. By applying a fresh mind to the problem, it was often possible to make a quick improvement.

During that week, the local bush telegraph must have been working overtime and on the Saturday, I played my first game for Ballymena. Syd Millar, a friend from the 1959 Lions tour, was the contact and he also organised a chauffeur in the shape of Irish scrum-half Jonny Moffett to drive me to the game. The following Saturday, in Edinburgh, we were on opposite sides when Scotland played Ireland, from which I emerged on the winning side, 16–8. On any free Sundays I had in Ireland, Jonnie took me under his wing and he introduced me to playing squash and watching Gaelic football as well as managing the odd game of golf.

Having won our two home games in the Five Nations, we headed to Twickenham for an attempt to win an elusive Triple Crown. No one needed reminding that 'Wilson Shaw's Match' in 1938 was the last time Scotland had been successful. Although we had lost our opening game in Paris, our pack had developed into a well-balanced and formidable unit.

Mike Campbell-Lamerton had appeared from nowhere playing for the Combined Services and he formed a hefty second row with Frans ten Bos, the first Dutchman to play for Scotland before Tim Visser was capped in 2012. Our front row of Hugh McLeod, Norman Bruce and Dave Rollo were now in their third season together and were bested by no one, including the South Africans who were renowned for their scrummaging. A new back row of the experienced Ken Smith and newcomers John Douglas and Ken Ross added mobility and ball-playing skills to the stability of the front five.

Losing the match 6–0 was a huge disappointment. Mike Campbell-Lamerton called off on the Friday and instead of replacing like for like, John Douglas was moved forward to the second row, Ken Smith was moved from blind side to No. 8, Ken Ross was moved from open to blind side and a new cap, John Brash, was brought in at open side. The selectors effectively made four changes when only one was necessary and the balance in the pack was seriously disrupted. With three of the pack playing out of position and with a new cap they were unable to replicate the form they had shown against Wales and Ireland. It was particularly hard on John Brash, who was a very good open side wing forward and was never selected again.

Despite all the above, it was a very close game and had we taken all our chances it could have been won. In the event it was just another addition to the lengthening Twickenham tale of woe.

Back in Edinburgh, arrangements for our wedding had been going on apace. On Easter Monday, two weeks after the Calcutta Cup, Doreen and I were married at St Andrew's Church, Juniper Green, Edinburgh, almost seven years to the day since our first date. Doreen had three bridesmaids – Catherine, Eddie McKeating's long-term girlfriend and future wife; Elsie, my sister; and Yvonne, a college friend from Dundee. My brother Ronnie was my best man and I had three ushers – Brian, Doreen's younger brother; Eddie McKeating; and Gordon Waddell. There was one unintended consequence in that Eddie had to turn down an invitation to play for the Barbarians on their Easter tour to south Wales. It was understood that, having declined the opportunity once, no one ever received a second invitation, which meant he missed out on a well-deserved honour.

The highlight of our reception at the George Hotel was the very witty toast to the bride and groom proposed by Norman Mair. Norman, who became a legend as a rugby and golf writer with the *Scotsman*, was already a mentor to us both and he did us proud. He described it as a marriage of equals but I feel that that did less than justice to Doreen.

I was lucky to escape the reception fully clad and shod but we were both still shedding confetti in the foyer of the St Enochs Hotel in Glasgow where we had an overnight stop.

The following morning, we caught an early flight to Belfast from where we set off to explore the north of Ireland. Our first day took us through Londonderry and on to an overnight stay at Carrigart on the north Donegal coast. We continued round the north and down the west coast of Donegal to spend the night in the town of Donegal itself. It was a wonderfully peaceful drive on quiet roads with the postage-stamp sized enclosed fields and the total lack of machinery the most memorable features.

On day three, we got as far south as the seaport town of Sligo where we abandoned the car for the afternoon and enjoyed an exploration of the pretty town on foot. The following morning, we turned east heading for Banbridge and to introduce Doreen to the Downshire Arms Hotel, where we were to stay for the next few weeks. En route we stayed the night in Virginia at a very nice hotel with a golf course within its own grounds.

By mid-morning on the Saturday, we had dropped off our luggage at the Downshire Arms and were heading for Ravenhill to spectate at the semi-finals of the Ulster Cup, which were due to be played that afternoon as a double header.

As Ballymena had been drawn to play CIYMS in the second game, we were in no hurry and slipped into the stand just after half-time in the first game. Much to our joint embarrassment, I was spotted by an eagle-eyed Ballymena committeeman who was insistent that I should play. I was not keen, partly because I had no kit and partly because a young lad was already stripped and raring to go. I never found out the full story. It is possible that the young lad was already overwhelmed by the occasion and happy to step down. Anyway, I was persuaded to play and fortunately his boots were a tolerably good fit.

We won a typical cup-tie narrowly and after a bath and a beer I was told that Doreen had gone off with some of the girls, including Enid, Syd Millar's girlfriend, and that we would all meet up later at the dance back at the clubhouse in Ballymena. When we did eventually meet, my bride of five days was not impressed by the fact that she and the other girls, left to their own devices, had been forced to stand at the side of the road and thumb a lift to reach Ballymena. Male chauvinism was still alive and well in Northern Ireland back then.

On the other hand, there was nothing wrong with their hospitality. One Wednesday evening I played in an Invitation XV at Lurgan to mark the opening of a new clubhouse. At the dinner after the game, Doreen was made welcome as the only female present and Noel Henderson, an Ireland regular in the 1950s and brother-in-law of my boyhood hero, Jackie Kyle, sang 'A Scottish Soldier' especially for her.

My assignment in Banbridge was coming to an end, but lasted just long enough to fit in the Ulster Cup final. Without knowing much about Ulster club rugby, I thought that we had a team, including a young Willie John McBride, capable of winning quite comfortably. Collegians obviously had other thoughts and they won a good hard-fought cup-tie 6–3.

Above left: With mother and father on brother Ronnie's Christening Day.
Above right: With Granddad Scotland and Granny Forbes.

With Ronnie and Elsie.

Heriot's School 1st XV 1952/53. *Back row:* Mr G Blamire, JA Fleming, DA Munro, BE Lynch, JC Henderson, IEA Palmer, CJ Trotter. *Front row:* SW McGregor, KJF Scotland, DS McGregor, AG Livingstone (vice-captain), J Carracher (captain), IG Noble, IC Thomson, E McKeating, JL Boak.

On the terracing at Goldenacre sixty years later. Ian Palmer, myself, Brendan Lynch and Derrick Munro.

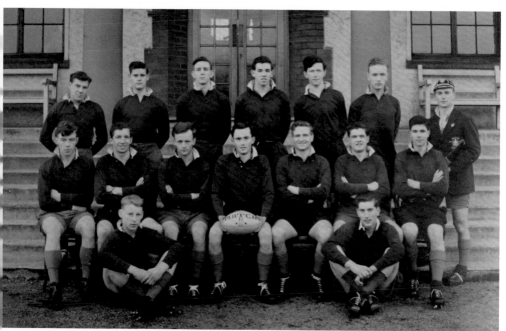

Edinburgh Schools, 1952. *Back row:* GT Vaughan (Stewart's), AG Livingstone (Heriot's), EJ Ireland (RHS), JCM Hill (Melville), G Grahamslaw (RHS), JB Lacey (RHS), JJ Gibb (Watson's) *Middle row:* A Wright (RHS), A McLaren (Watson's), G Sharp (Stewart's), CG McGulloch (Melville), J Carracher (Heriot's), WM Collins (Watson's), GC Lennox (Melville) *Front row:* KJF Scotland (Heriot's), NJ McGlasson (Melville)

London Scottish Schools XV, 1954. *Back row:* PDH Nichols (Harrow), JDD MacBean (Fettes), JB Neill (Edinburgh Academy) *Middle row:* DW Horne (Fettes), IR Gibbons (Glasgow High School), NRC Marr (Marlborough), JDS Hay (Bedford), GH Waddell (Fettes), KJF Scotland (Heriot's), HB Curtis (Leys) *Front row:* E McKeating (Heriot's), CH Wood (KCS Wimbledon), HJ Kirsop (Fettes), KND Ruxton (Loretto), CRM Bannerman (Merchiston), FHD Walker (Edinburgh Academy)

Heriot's School Cricket 1st XI, 1955. *Back row:* Mr LL Mitchell, RJ Scotland, GR McG. Wright, DS McCracken, PJR O'Malley, DP Brown (scorer) *Front row:* HK More, EH Tainsh, KJF Scotland, E McKeating, GF Goddard, CJ Horton, A Ramsay. See page 15 for various honours.

Heriot's School Seven 1954/55. *Back row:* IH Moyes, HS Jamieson, DS McCracken, JBH Wilson, A Ramsay
Front row: KJF Scotland, E McKeating (captain), DK Kelly.
Winners at: Paisley Grammar School, Hillhead High School, Murrayfield, Goldenacre.
Eddie McKeating, Drew Ramsay and myself were in the Heriot's FP Seven which won at Melrose in 1957 and 1958.

Army v Navy, Twickenham 3 March 1956.
Back row: M Hartley, R Roe, TGAH Peart, HM Inglis, EJS Michie, KRF Bearne, T Thomas, I Southward
Middle row: NS Bruce, AB Edwards, DW Shuttleworth, WE Townsend, DS Gilbert-Smith
Front row: KJF Scotland, J Regan. Eleven of the team played international rugby, including one in rugby league.

On parade with the Duke of Edinburgh and some serious top brass.

My first cap, France v Scotland, Stade Colombes, 12 January 1957. *Back row:* Mr LM Boundy (England, referee), JS Swan, IAA MacGregor, JWY Kemp, AR Smith, T Elliot, JT Greenwood, EJS Michie, GD Stevenson, A Robson, RKG MacEwen *Front:* E McKeating, HF McLeod, AF Dorward, ML Grant, KJF Scotland

1TR Royal Signals with the Army Cup in 1957. There was one Regular Officer in the team with the rest being national servicemen from all over the UK, including Jim Smith from the Royal High School in Edinburgh.

Left: Entering Tynecastle for physio treatment.

Right: Pictured with my Scotland crickt cap.

In action for Cambridge against Oxford in 1958, I'm in John Young's sights (a Lions colleague a year later) with Malcolm Phillips, an England centre, and Gordon Waddell awaiting developments.

Scoring for Cambridge against the Steele-Bodgers qith Arthur Smith on top and Robin Chisholm, my competition for the Scotland full back position, hidden underneath. Arthur got his revenge later in the game when he beat me on the outside with his trademark change of pace.

The 1959 Lions tour party. *Back row:* D Hewitt, MJ Price, PB Jackson, AA Mulligan, HJ Morgan, BGM Wood *Third row:* S Miller, TR Prosser, NH Brophy, GK Smith, A Ashcroft, GH Waddell, TJ Davies *Second row:* WA Mulcahy, J Faull, WR Evans, RWD Marques, RH Williams, AJF O'Reilly, S Coughtrie, NAA Murphy *Seated:* HF McLeod, MC Thomas, AW Wilson (Hon. Manager), AR Dawson(Captain), OB Glasgow (Hon. Secretary), J Butterfield, BV Meredith *In front:* REG Jeeps, JRC Young, KJF Scotland, ABW Risman, MAF English *Insert:* P Horrocks-Taylor, W Patterson

Captaining the Lions against Otago at Carisbrook in Dunedin.

A great picture, but this try agianst the Maori at Eden Park was disallowed for a so-called 'adjustment', which was then illegal. There was no doubt in my mind that it was a perfectly good try under any interpretation of the laws. A pity in a way because that was the only game on tour when we failed to score a try.

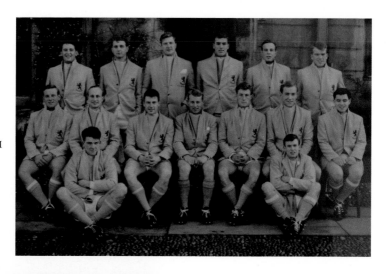

Cambridge University XV 1960/61. *Back row:* RCB Michaelson, RB Collier, VSJ Harding, B Thomas, BA Dovey, DFB Wrench *Middle row:* M Lord, A Godson, MR Wade, KJF Scotland, MT Wetson, JC Brash, TC Wintle *Front row:* GH Waddell, WM Bussey

The Cambridge team that won the 1960 Melrose 7s. *Back row:* Mike Wetson, Cameron Boyle, John Brash, Alan Godson. *In front:* Ronnie Thomson, myself and Gordon Waddell.

Winning the 1960 Middlesex 7s at Twickenham with London Scottish. Iain Laughland is holding the trophy, supported by Jim Shackleton, Robin Marshall, Don Trow, Ian Reid, David Hayburn and myself.

Artthur Smith scores against Wales in 1961 after my pass releases him down the right wing. 'Intuitive genius,' The *Scotsman*'s Jack Dunn called it – 'a peach of a pass.'

You can't see me in this shot, but as Dewi Webb races away down the wing in the 1961 clash against Wales, I made one of the best tackles in my career to stop him from scoring in the corner.

Achieving the third (and greatest) of my life aims: marrying Doreen in 1961.

Leicester Tigers, 1961/62. *Back row:* RJ Barr (Hon. Secretary), D Bolesworth (Hon. Team Secretary), JA Allen, G Hopkins, C Shephard, JM Jones, R Rowell, P Riley, BTC Small, DW Bird, G Cherry, RL Bedingfield (President) *Middle row:* MR Walker, MR Wade, JP Horrocks-Taylor, CG Martin (captain), KJF Scotland, F Chawner, G Almey, D Senior *Front row:* DJ Matthews, L Tatham, IM Gibson, HV White, NJ Drake-Lee

Captaining Scotland at Twickenham in 1963. *Back row:* Mr TE Grierson (Touch Judge), DF Blaikie, DM White, BC Henderson, S Coughtrie, MJ Campbell-Lamerton, FH ten Bos, JP Fisher, KI Ross, JB Neill, DMD Rollo Mr DG Walters (Referee) *Front row:* RJC Glasgow, NS Bruce, KJF Scotland, C Elliot, RH Thomson

North Midlands v the All Blacks, January 1964. *Back row:* IC Spence (Gordonians), GP Hill (Gordonians), IC Wood (Gordonians), MGH Gibb (Aberdeen Grammar School FP) Middle row: D A Bryce (Dunfermline), AW Sinclair (Perthshire Accies), RJC Glasgow (Dunfermline), AGD Whyte (Gordonians), GP Pashley (Perthshire Accies), JB Steven (Madras College FP) *Front row:* IG McRae (Gordonians), KJF Scotland (Aberdeenshire), BW Brown (St Andrews University), CP Carter (St Andrews University), CC McLeod (Madras College FP). North Midlands 3 New Zealand 15

Captaining Aberdeenshire. *Back row:* M Brewer, A Tucker, G Roberts, A Morgan, J Sutherland *Middle row:* J Drummond, J McMorran, C McMillan, A McLachlan, M Calloway, A Skene, I Robertson, Mr JC Williams *Front row:* B Stephen, D Millar, J Snape, K Scotland, M Reid, A Massie, D Macpherson.
I'm wearing the Canterbury jersey I was given after being stretchered off in Christchurch.

Heriot's eight Scotland full backs. *In front:* Andy Irvine and Dan Drysdale.
Standing: Ian Thomson, Colin Blaikie, Jim Kerr, Tommy Gray, myself and Ian Smith.

The Bottomleys, Jarvis's, McKeatings and Scotlands ready to drive off.

Lions reunion during the 2007 Rugby World Cup in Paris. *Back row:* JRC Young, HT Morris, CC Meredith, RJ Robins, TJ Davies, HF McLeod, MAF English, KJF Scotland, REG Jeeps *Middle row:* F Sykes, BV Meredith, WA Mulcahy, RJ McLaughlin, RWD Marques, NH Brophy, GK Smith, NA Murphy, AB Risman *Front row:* C Pedlow, J Matthews, BW Williams, JS McCarthy, AR Dawson, AJF O'Reilly, CI Morgan, J Kyle, WPC Davies, D Hewitt
Not pictured: S Millar, B Williams, J Faull

The family gathered in Brodick for our Golden Wedding anniversary.

Golden Wedding family foursome with Iain, Alistair and Robin at Shiskine Golf Club.

The Norwegian Connection with the ladies in national costume.

TEN

BECOMING A TIGER

On the day after the cup final, we flew out of Belfast and spent the night in the Station Hotel, Wolverhampton. This was only significant because Sunday 23 April was the date of the 1961 Census and future generations of Scotlands might well find it difficult to trace us to the only night we ever spent in Wolverhampton.

We had a week before my next assignment was due to start in a factory producing caravan windows in Erdington, a suburb of Birmingham. Priorities for the week were to become mobile and to find somewhere to live. With all our joint savings we bought a minivan, 273DOX, and eventually we found a suitable flat on Lichfield Road, Walsall.

As the assignment this time was in work measurement, I also had to find time to be given a crash course on the use of a stopwatch by Phil Horrocks-Taylor. I had followed Phil into the Royal Signals at Catterick and to university at Cambridge, and I now caught up with him on a beaten-earth shop floor in Wolverhampton. Appearances were deceptive because the factory was the largest manufacturer of hospital beds in the UK.

As Phil explained it, in theory the work looked pretty straight forward, but I was to find out there were many pitfalls for the inexperienced in practice.

On the Saturday, we ran-in the minivan at thirty miles an hour down the newly opened M1 from Watford Gap on our way to Twickenham for the finals of the Middlesex Sevens. Ronnie Thompson on the wing was the only change in the winning London Scottish side from the previous season. His quarter-miler's pace and stamina added a cutting edge throughout a gruelling afternoon. On the way to the final, we beat three very fit and quick student sevens – Emmanuel College, Cambridge; St Luke's College, Exeter; and Loughborough College. In contrast, in the final, we met one of the guest sides, Stewart's College FP from Edinburgh. Brought up with all the guile and know-how of the Scottish Borders sevens circuit, they had very experienced players in the Sharp brothers, Gordon Robertson and John Douglas. I quote from a press cutting: 'One import England can gladly encourage is Scottish seven-a-side rugby. In an electrifying final to the Middlesex Sevens, on a perfect afternoon in front of a crowd of 40,000, London Scottish defeated their fellows from north of the border by 20 points to 6.'

The margin of four tries to two is a better indication of the closeness of the final. I remember well one incident from the match. It is odd that in front of a big crowd and with other players on the pitch, I was conscious of only one other person. From about our own twenty-five, I made a break on a diagonal line and was chased the whole way by John Douglas. I never felt that he was going to catch me but he did force me out towards the corner to make the conversion more difficult. Lung-bursting for both of us but very good tactics on his part.

Back in Erdington on the Monday morning, I made my first solo appearance on a shop floor with stop-watch in hand. It was a terrifying experience. I remember thinking that I would rather have been standing under a high ball with a pack of forwards fast approaching than where I was at that moment. In theory, if the idea is sold well, work measurement should have benefits for both the management and the workforce. As I was soon to discover, the management were terrified of the men on the shop floor and had made no effort to explain the overall benefits. Thus, I was a management tool, there to help exploit the men and I met with a lot of open hostility. After two weeks the company moved into a new purpose-built factory in Tamworth and for the rest of the assignment relationships gradually improved. Once the employees realised that part of the end result could be productivity bonuses for them they became more interested. I came to enjoy the work and to do a 'Day Study', i.e. timing one man throughout his eight-hour day, was an interesting and enlightening experience.

We settled quickly into Walsall. Doreen got a job as a supply teacher of domestic science locally and we discovered that it did not take long to get out of the Black Country to the countryside at Cannock Chase or to the cathedral city of Lichfield. It was hard for Doreen without any friends in the area, but we did exchange visits with Phil and Julia Horrocks-Taylor in Wolverhampton.

One weekend I was drawn to the local cricket club with the prospect of watching Tom Graveney batting. He was taking a mandatory year out of county cricket as he changed his allegiance from Gloucester to Worcester and was playing for a club in the Birmingham league. Or not playing as it turned out that day. I never did see that stylish batsman in action, but it did introduce me to Walsall Cricket Club, where I managed to play the fullest season's cricket since my first year in Catterick. The standard of cricket was high and the spectators were partisan and noisy. Walsall had a 'Shed' which was as intimidating to the opposition as were the Sheds at Gloucester and Redruth rugby grounds. The intimidation was continued by the Walsall opening bowlers.

John Aldridge, the club professional who was kept out of the Worcester county side by the well-known pair of Len Coldwell and Jack Flavell, started at one end and there was no respite at the other end from a young David Brown who went on to play for England. To carry on the intimidation theme, I felt much the same way just fielding at first slip.

Over the season, I played as many games for the seconds as I did for the firsts but one of the pleasures was to play at some very scenic grounds, particularly I remember Kidderminster and the natural amphitheatre at Old Hill.

By the middle of August, with the assignment in Tamworth showing no signs of coming to an early end, I had to decide where would be the best and most convenient place to play rugby the following season. The fact that Doreen was now pregnant also had to be fitted into the equation. Taking up where I had left off last season before moving to Northern Ireland and travelling to London to play for Scottish was not really an option. The nearest first-class club to Walsall was Moseley, in Birmingham, but I had absolutely no connections there. With the company I worked for based there, Leicester was really the obvious choice. A slight hesitation was that Leicester already had an England international full-back in Mick Gavins playing for them. That dilemma was resolved when Mick decided to join Moseley.

I had never enjoyed playing against Leicester. The ground at Welford Road is intimidating with the partisan crowd seemingly almost on the pitch but I soon came to appreciate playing behind their mean pack of forwards.

The daily commute from Walsall to Tamworth was pleasant in the summer and could be varied by taking minor roads. As summer progressed through autumn to winter, driving both to and from work in the dark became a chore and at times a hazard. The West Midlands' climate was damp and in winter regularly developed into a freezing fog.

The decision to join Leicester also meant a fifty-mile cross country journey on a Saturday for home games. Having Doreen for company made driving to play rugby matches much more enjoyable. From the start of the season through to early December, as well as ten home games at Leicester, we travelled four times to London with single journeys to Blundellsands, Gloucester and Cambridge. The highlight should have been the trip back to Cambridge who still had most of the team I had played with the previous season. Had there been an HIA (Head Injury Assessment) protocol in place then I would have been off the field before half-time. As no one had heard of such a thing then, I played to the end of the game, but instead of a few beers with my old friends I was sent to bed nursing a nasty headache.

By the beginning of December 1961, life was getting complicated. Doreen had arranged to have our baby in Edinburgh, due in early February, and my assignment in Tamworth was coming to an end with a move to a shoe factory in Northampton likely to occur early in the New Year. In mid-December, we left the flat in Walsall and moved in with Doreen's parents back in Edinburgh and Doreen began her wait, impatiently, for nature to take its course while I dotted back and forth to England, keeping my job and rugby season alive.

Fortunately, for a four-week period around Christmas and New Year, the three rugby matches I played were in Edinburgh – two national trials followed by France at Murrayfield in the 1962 Five Nations. There was one blip, however. The previous year I had played for the Barbarians against Leicester in the annual Christmas fixture. This year I was due to reverse sides and play against the Barbarians. I had left the minivan at Birmingham airport before Christmas and was due to fly down on the morning of the game. I was assured the night before the game that it would definitely be played. No problem, they had heaters going all night to keep the frost at bay. I made it to Birmingham as planned, but overnight snow and severe frost had made the roads extremely hazardous.

In the days before mobile phones it was very difficult under these circumstances to keep in touch. The first time I stopped at a telephone box, I said that I was on my way but that I was struggling to be there in time for the kick-off. At further stops, all I got from the rugby club was an engaged line. When I eventually arrived, in a lather, having missed the kick-off time, I discovered that their heating arrangements had been inadequate and the game was off. This time the minivan was abandoned in Leicester as I caught the first train back to Edinburgh.

Having brought in the New Year in Edinburgh, I went back south to start the new assignment in Northampton. I was staying in a hotel there when on Tuesday 23 January, I received an early morning call to tell me that overnight I had become the father of a baby boy. Apart from a breakdown in Wetherby, I have no memory of the hectic journey up the old A1 but it was a great relief to arrive at the Elsie Inglis Maternity Hospital in Edinburgh just as all the proud fathers were being allowed into the wards for the evening visiting hour. Doreen had had a long hard labour and although tired she looked radiant and Robin was the bonniest baby boy ever.

After a celebratory meal with the four delighted first-time grandparents, I caught the sleeper to Kettering to be back at work the following morning.

Finding somewhere to live as soon as Doreen and Robin were fit to travel south was now a priority. In the meantime, I moved into a bachelor flat with two friends from Cambridge, Ronnie Hoare and Roger Prideaux, and the captain of the Saints Cricket Club, Pat Heron. Rodger was secretary of, and playing for, the Northamptonshire County Cricket Club and I was accommodated on a mattress on his bedroom floor. On Thursday 25 January, they organised an impromptu Burns Supper in Robin's honour.

On the Friday night I was on the sleeper back up to Edinburgh to get my first experience of the joys of parenthood. To get some exercise, as opposed to sitting in trains, I had arranged to get a game at stand-off for Heriot's 3rd XV against an Edinburgh University XV. The standard of the game was no better or worse than was to be expected, but I was wryly amused, in the communal bath afterwards, at how critical they were about the performances of the Scottish team in the recent game against France.

Losing 11–3 to a good French side who were going through a run of successful seasons was no disgrace, but the result did less than justice to our forwards who more than held their own, but got insufficient support from the backs.

In our next game against Wales at Cardiff Arms Park, the forwards kept up their good work leading the way to a first victory in Wales for twenty-five years and the first in Cardiff since 1927. The previous win in 1937 had been played in Swansea.

The game was played in continuous wind and rain. Our forwards dominated and scored the two tries which allowed us to win by 8–3.

Three weeks later in Dublin, with a better balanced team performance, we won by the slightly flattering margin of 20 points to 6, setting up a Triple Crown possibility against England at Murrayfield.

Although Scotland had won a Triple Crown in 1938, no team since 1933 had won in Wales and Ireland in the same season to play the decider at home against England.

After the 3–3 draw, the third in the last five games against England, the mood in the dressing room was as quiet as I can ever remember. It was generally known within the team that Hugh McLeod and Arthur Smith had decided that this was their last game for Scotland. It was Hugh's ninth and Arthur's seventh game against England without a win and we all knew how much it meant to them. I felt the disappointment more than anyone else as I missed two kickable penalties towards the end of the game which would undoubtedly have won us the match. In retrospect, had I kicked one of those goals the team of seasons 1961 and 1962 would have been more than just a footnote in the annals of Scottish rugby.

Apart from the odd change for injury, the front five played throughout both seasons. Hugh McLeod, Norman Bruce and Dave Rollo would stand comparison with any front row produced by Scotland. The second row of Mike Campbell-Lamerton and Frans ten Bos weighed in at over 34 stone and were described in the press at that time as monstrous. In the back row, two mobile ball-players in John Douglas and Kenny Ross were complemented, in 1961, by Ken Smith and, in 1962, by Ronnie Glasgow, who were both quick and physical.

The backs were nothing like as settled. Arthur Smith – who captained the team both years – and I were the only two who played in all eight games. Iain Laughland played seven games, four in the centre and three at stand-off, with Gordon Waddell at stand-off in the other five matches. Sharing the centre positions with Iain, more or less equally, were Eddie McKeating, Joe McPartlin and George Stevenson, while Ronnies Cowan and Thompson shared the other wing position. At scrum-half, the games were shared by Stan Coughtrie, Alec Hastie, Tremayne Rodd and Brian Shillinglaw, who all brought unique individual skills to their position.

Winning the Triple Crown for the first time since 1938 would have been a suitable reward for that group of players.

Scottish rugby had moved on from the dismal early 1950s record of seventeen successive defeats. Although it is only a rough measure of success, it is worth noting that ten of the above squad played at some stage in their careers for the Lions, with Arthur Smith captain in South Africa in 1962 and Mike Campbell-Lamerton captain in New Zealand in 1966.

Earlier in the year, I had decided that I would not be available for selection for the summer Lions Tour to South Africa. I had missed a Barbarian tour there in 1957 because it coincided with my first-year exams, and also a Scottish visit in 1960 which clashed with my final degree exams.

While I was sorry to miss another opportunity to visit one of the great powers in world rugby I had no doubt that I was making the correct decision. My priority was now to provide for my family and concentrate on my business career.

Meanwhile, having negotiated a six-month let, the three of us had moved into a very nice house in the rural setting of a village called Long Buckby about ten miles outside Northampton and close to what was then the northern extremity of the M1 at the Watford Gap.

Despite family and business now coming first, in the four weeks after the Calcutta Cup, I played four games in Leicester and one each at Llanelli, Birkenhead and Liverpool. On the fifth weekend I went on the Barbarians' Easter tour and played against Cardiff, Swansea and Newport.

On the next, and final, Saturday of the season, I was due to play for London Scottish at Twickenham to defend the Middlesex Sevens Cup, which we had won for the previous two seasons. However, my charmed luck ran out. Doreen was confined to bed and I had to call off on the Saturday morning and belatedly come to face the reality of family responsibility.

Fortunately, I wasn't missed. Iain Laughland moved to stand-off with Tremayne Rodd coming in at scrum-half and not only did they retain the cup but they went on to win the following season as well to make it four-in-a-row.

*

The highlight of the summer of 1962 spent in rural Northamptonshire was an invitation to a Garden Party at

Buckingham Palace. En route we left Robin in Beaconsfield with Alistair and Moira Hamilton, former neighbours of Doreen's in Kingsknowe.

We were wryly amused to drive our minivan through the main gates of the palace and park in the front courtyard.

The guests were assembled in a long corridor prior to being introduced to the Queen and the Duke of Edinburgh. We were third in the queue behind Sir Stanley Matthews and his wife, and Michael and Angela Bonallack. Other guests we recognised were Kenneth More, Christine Truman, Richard Attenborough, Sir Bernard Lovell and David Broome. We also met up with Lloyd Williams, the Welsh scrum-half, and his wife.

Also during the summer, I played cricket irregularly for the Northampton Saints along with my ex house mates Ronnie Hoare and Pat Heron.

Fortunately, the end of my assignment in the shoe factory in Northampton and our six-month rental in Long Buckby coincided. Work involved a return to the caravan windows factory in Tamworth and after a frantic search we found very nice accommodation in Tudor Hill, Sutton Coldfield. Being adjacent to Sutton Park came in handy for pram pushing and occasional training runs. It also allowed us to renew our friendship with Peter and Eileen Robbins.

The daily commute of ten miles to Tamworth was pleasant and fairly quiet but the weekend travelling became onerous. In the first fourteen weeks of the 1962/63 season, I played in Bath, Sheffield, London, Swansea, Coventry, Cheltenham, Oxford, Gloucester and Newcastle as well as seven home games in Leicester. For the home games at Welford Road it was a pleasant family outing, but for the rest I was travelling on my own.

The game in Swansea was particularly memorable. As any rugby player will tell you, going to play in Wales is never easy. No matter what the level, from minor club to the Barbarians, there is never an easy game. The combination of rugby being the Welsh national game, the players' inherent pride and ability, and the noisy partisan crowds all make any win in Wales something to celebrate. And we won by 29 points to 6.

'Swansea demoralised by Leicester' read the headline to David Onllwyn Brace's match report, below which he wrote:

Leicester's victory at the famous St Helens ground was as convincing as the score suggested,' he wrote, 'for they played magnificent football to demoralise thoroughly and completely outclass the home side in every department.

'Most encouraging was the manner in which the Tigers set about winning, for they handed out a lesson in all the finer arts of rugby football. It was refreshing to see hard, vigorous yet clean forward play supported by three-quarter movements of the highest order.

All Leicester's attacks were inevitably based around their fly-half, Horrocks-Taylor, who played superbly in attack and defence. It has been many a day since a Swansea crowd has seen such a fine exposition, for the English international produced almost every gambit in the outside-half's repertoire.

Extremely well serviced by his scrum-half, White, Horrocks-Taylor repeatedly set his line in motion with a fluent pass that was an object lesson for all young players. His breaks, perfectly timed, always paid rich dividends while his kicking strategically placed in attack, and face-saving in defence, was always a thorn in Swansea's flesh. His combination with the centre three-quarters, Gibson and Cooper, themselves no mean attackers, was a particular feature and their willingness to try the unorthodox was much appreciated by the crowd.

The game was a personal triumph, too, for full-back Scotland, Leicester's Scottish international. In addition to contributing 17 points to his side's total with his accurate place-kicking, his periodic excursions into the three-quarter line added thrust and sparkle, while in the more ordinary task of full-back play he illustrated that he still has no equal as a catcher and kicker of the ball.

Well though these two internationals played, this victory was essentially that of a team effort, a team extremely well equipped fore and aft. First, Leicester had the essential basic ingredient of team-work – a big, mighty yet mobile pack who managed with great success to give their thrustful three-quarters a fairly constant supply of the ball, particularly from the loose mauls where they foraged with rare zeal and enthusiasm.

The Leicester skipper, Martin, an enterprising lock-forward, set a fine example and led his well-drilled pack with skill. Prominent in support were the prop-forward, Drake-Lee, second-row men Rowell and Jones, and back-row men Small and Matthews.

Swansea were the first and last to score; Faull kicked a penalty in the opening few minutes and centre three-quarter Powell scored a try late in the second half. In between Leicester tries were scored by Horrocks-Taylor (2), Drake-Lee and Gibson. Scotland converted all these in addition to kicking three fine penalty goals.

It was the sort of game that fully justified all the perceived benefits of team sport – all fifteen players playing to the very best of their ability, having confidence in each other, never losing focus and, of course, enjoying an after-match refreshment together and with the opposition.

*

The work I was doing I enjoyed. I also felt that it was worthwhile. Low productivity in all types of industries was making British products non-competitive. However, working on short-term contracts with changes being made often with little warning was not conducive to bringing up a young family. Consequently, I started looking for a change of job, preferably based in Scotland. I knew that low-productivity was at least as big a problem in Scotland and I also looked forward to finishing off my rugby career with Heriot's.

At the beginning of December, I accepted a job with an Edinburgh-based firm of management consultants. To work out my notice, I was allocated an assignment in a shoe factory in Norwich. So it was back to Mum and Dad in Edinburgh for Doreen, and Robin.

ELEVEN

SCOTLAND'S SCOTLAND

I think it is worth giving a bit of background to the 1963 Five Nations Championship. At the line-out, the offside line was an extension of the gap between the two sets of forwards. At a scrum, as long as a player was behind the ball he was onside. From first phase possession there was therefore no incentive for the backs to pass. There was also no restriction on putting the ball out of play anywhere on the pitch. (The so-called 'Australian Dispensation' which meant loss of ground for kicks to touch outside the 25 yard line was still a few years away.)

The winter of 1962/63 was one of the coldest in recent memory. From mid-December to the end of February there was virtually no club rugby played, which meant that all the players were short of match practice. France were the dominant team at that time having come out on top the previous four years and not having lost in Paris since 1958.

The French game, then, was always our first, and that year it was to be played in Paris. We still had the nucleus of the – by Scottish standards – successful sides of 1961 and 1962, except that, as predicted, both our most experienced players, Hugh

McLeod and Arthur Smith, had retired and ex-captain Gordon Waddell had departed to Stanford Business School in America. The biggest decision the selectors had to make was who to replace Gordon at stand-off. Two young players, Jimmy Blake of the Royal High and Drew Broach of Hawick, were widely tipped but the Big Five went with the experience of Iain Laughland. As the next most long-serving, I was selected as captain, continuing a run of former Cambridge University players. I followed Gordon Waddell, who was captain five times, and Arthur Smith, ten times, from 1959 to 1962.

With no coaches at that time, I was largely responsible for our tactics. As it had been for the two years under Arthur Smith, my principal sounding board was Norman Mair, now writing for *The Scotsman*. We concluded that there were two main reasons for France's success. Their forwards had learned from the recent visit of the Springboks to create good second phase possession and without that advantage their backs never attempted any handling movements. Our tactical approach was to match them up front and only to move the ball in the backs if we got really good possession.

The game itself was a bit bizarre. In early January, Paris had been experiencing the same very cold weather as the UK and the pitch had been belatedly covered in an inadequately thin layer of straw. To make the pitch playable the straw was set on fire, so when the teams emerged from the underground changing rooms, we were faced with a black rather than a green surface. In those days there was no such thing as a pre-match warm-up so the appearance of the pitch came as a bit of a shock. It's doubtful if the pitch was ever playable and it became harder as the game progressed.

Our tactics worked to the extent that we won. Playing against the elements in the first half, we conceded a penalty and a drop goal. In the second half, with our forwards increasingly taking control, I equalised, again with a drop goal and a penalty. With the last play of the game, Iain Laughland tried to drop a goal, which although wide of the posts bounced wildly on the hard ground into the delighted hands of our right wing, Ronnie Thomson. It was great anticipation on his part because he touched down well wide of the left-hand post.

Three weeks later, and adopting the same tactics as in Paris, where we had inflicted on France their first defeat at Colombes in the Five Nations for five seasons, we were beaten by 6 points to 0 at Murrayfield by Wales. This was the infamous match of 111 lines-out, still known, I am very happy to say, as 'Rowlands' Match'. I have never discussed the game with Clive Rowlands, but I have read him being quoted as saying that the poor weather conditions were largely to blame. My reading of the game was that both teams were adopting a no-risk strategy, dictated by the laws at that time – which allowed a kicker to kick straight into touch anywhere on the field and a line-out would be awarded where the ball crossed the line. As I say, we'd beaten France by kicking a lot and hoped to repeat that. It was a very frustrating day but to be honest we'd wanted to play a similar sort of game to the Welsh only they'd been better at it.

Against Ireland at Murrayfield three weeks later, and with much the same approach, we won by a Stan Coughtrie penalty to nil. For this game, I was moved to stand-off and the selectors brought in Colin Blaikie, making him the sixth Herioter to play full-back for Scotland. The line-out count was reduced to eighty-three but if the sixty-one scrums were added, there was not much time for open play. Both games must have been dire to watch but Test matches are only there to be won and I found both games absorbing, if not exciting, to play in.

In the press at the time much of the criticism was levelled at the selectors. They were indeed wholly responsible for picking the team. For example, as captain, I was never asked what I felt about being moved up to stand-off. That was their decision. However, the Big Five had little or no say in how the game was played on the pitch. The perception was that the selectors picked a team to play a certain style. The fact was that it was the players who dictated the style. This was a fundamental weakness only overcome by the introduction of coaches.

Strangely, it was never the captain who gave the final tactical rallying call to the team before going out to play – but the president of the SRU, or the chairman of the selectors, who would come into the dressing room, call for silence and then cry, 'Fire and fucking fury!'

It seems to have been a call-to-arms that was passed down from one president or chairman of selectors to another and experienced by generations of Scotland players. Quite why it became such a tradition is a mystery.

Making use of the electric blanket at Murrayfield to give the players much-needed match practice, a game was arranged the week after the Ireland game. It was not a trial as such, with only four of the team who played against Ireland included. I was chosen at stand-off with Stan Coughtrie as my partner playing against the Hawick pairing of Drew Broach and Glen Turnbull. Many years later, Drew told me that he had been so disappointed not to be selected after his performance that day that he turned to a successful career in rugby league.

And so to Twickenham for the Calcutta Cup. I had no hang-ups about Twickenham as I had already played there about twenty times, mainly for the Army and Cambridge but also for and against Harlequins, who used it then as their home ground.

Doreen had received a very nice invitation from the Menzies family to have lunch at the Savoy along with transport to the game. Unfortunately, their bus was caught in a traffic jam and by the time my high-heeled, three-month pregnant wife had run the last half-mile she had missed the teams' introduction to the then Prime Minister, Harold Macmillan, and Scotland taking an eight-point lead.

In contrast to our three previous games, this one turned out to be a feast of running rugby. Our tactics were the same and the laws hadn't been changed, so why was this game different? I think that falling behind so early in the game forced England to take more risks. Richard Sharp, my opposite number, scored a delightful individual try from first phase possession, which should not in theory have been possible. At least three of us should have tackled him before he scored. A Peter Jackson try followed by a John Willcox touchline conversion sealed our fate. Altogether an exciting as well as an absorbing game to play in. Never having played in a winning team against England is the biggest regret of my rugby career, but I did have the consolation of learning that both captain's names are engraved on the Calcutta Cup.

TWELVE

ABERDEEN

On the second Monday after the game in Paris, having served my period of notice in Norwich, I presented myself for work at my new employer's office in Edinburgh. Without much in the way of introductions I was told that the company had just secured an exciting new contract in Aberdeen and that I was due to start there tomorrow. Having been living apart from Doreen and Robin for the best part of the last two months this was not the news that we wanted to hear.

The assignment was with Alexander Hall & Sons, the major all-trades building contractors in the north of Scotland. This was an office-based, organisation and methods study, rather than the largely factory-based work I had been involved with in England. As a result, I had a lot of contact with the managing director, Jack Hall. He soon became aware that I was urgently looking for accommodation to move the family up from Edinburgh and in typical Aberdeen fashion he had a friend who had a friend who just happened to have a flat to let, which wasn't yet on the market. In double quick time we moved into a comfortable modernised flat in Watson Street, in the Rosemount district of Aberdeen.

After three months, with the assignment due to finish, I was offered an interesting opportunity to stay in Aberdeen working for Halls. With no further consultancy work immediately on offer, this seemed an excellent chance to lay down some roots.

Halls wanted to take advantage of the boom in the demand for housing using the latest techniques in industrialised building. The company already had a state-of-the-art joinery factory, but had to start from scratch producing precast concrete. At the same time as I was recruited, a structural engineer, Bill Adamson, started with the company and a factory, fabricating structural steel units, was bought over as a going concern.

Over the next few months, Bill and I finished off the factory's existing order book, redesigned the factory layout and retrained the shop floor workers before producing our first precast concrete units. We also set up a ready-mix concrete plant.

Through an old school friend, Gilbert McIntosh, I was introduced to Aberdeenshire Cricket Club. I hadn't played a full season since my first year in the Army in 1956, but was interested in getting involved again. However, with family and business commitments and the amount of travelling involved playing counties cricket, I ended up making myself available for selection for Saturday games only and on the understanding that I didn't appear at net practice. On that basis, I played regularly as a wicketkeeper and middle order batsman.

For the Aberdeen trade holidays in mid-July, we stayed with Doreen's parents in Edinburgh. I had just taken possession of my first ever company car, one of the first Hillman Imps to come off the Linwood assembly line. It must also have been one of the very first to be written off. On the way to Gullane for a game of golf with my sounding-board friend Norman Mair, I came off second best at an unmarked suburban cross-roads in Morningside, with a Cleansing Department lorry. Neither I, nor my golf clubs, suffered lasting damage, but had there been a front seat passenger it would have been extremely serious. It was a salutary lesson and something I still think about driving on suburban roads.

With a career now developing in Aberdeen and another baby due in September, finding a permanent home became a priority. We were soon made aware of a suitable house, not yet on the market, and after one visit the deal was done. It was a typical granite-built four-bedroom detached house with a front door in Braemar Place and a back door onto Broomhill Road. By coincidence, the house was two along the street from where Ernie Michie, a former Army and Scotland colleague, had been brought up.

By the time of Iain's birth on 11 September, the house was sufficiently furnished and decorated, under the supervision of my mother-in-law, to welcome his arrival home from hospital.

*

At the start of the 1963/64 rugby season I had a problem. Would I travel to Edinburgh to play for Heriot's as I had originally intended or would I join a club in Aberdeen? With Doreen now looking after two small boys in a strange town and with no motorways and a ferry to contend with at Queensferry, I decided that realistically a regular commute to Edinburgh was just not practical.

In deciding to remain in Aberdeen, I came up against the uniquely Scottish problem of closed Former Pupil clubs. At that time, of the senior clubs, Gordonians were the better team but Aberdeen Grammar had the better fixture list. I would have been happy to play for either club but that was not on option as I hadn't attended either school.

Aberdeenshire and Aberdeen Wanderers were both long-established clubs but with few if any first-class fixtures. I joined Aberdeenshire solely on the basis that their captain, Ian Fletcher, took the trouble to track me down and sold me on the idea with his obvious enthusiasm and passion for his club.

For the first time since leaving Cambridge, I could now train twice a week with my teammates. In all the games I played for London Scottish, Ballymena and Leicester, I was never working closely enough to attend club training. To supplement the limited amount of training I managed on my own, I made a point of really pushing myself during games. As these games were all against first-class opposition, I had just about managed to stay match fit.

The Arctic weather conditions of early 1963 did nothing to help when I joined the club in late January, and it was not until well into April that it became possible to play a match. During the intervening period, the average numbers at training stayed steadily at three – a number greatly below that which patronised the upstairs bar in the George Hotel every Saturday evening.

After months of such masterly inactivity, it took a heroic effort to put a team on the field. It seemed to me, as a newcomer, that players had been borrowed from every club in Aberdeenshire and certainly our motley appearance might have confirmed that view.

That match introduced me to the delights of their changing room and pitch at the Chanonry. The amenities failed to match, by some way, those to which I had become accustomed at Cambridge or Leicester – it had one communal changing-room, for both teams and the referee, and was completely devoid of either artificial light or running water.

I also discovered that a knowledge of the contours of the pitch was always a distinct advantage to the home side and that the expression 'hanging lie' had a usage in rugby which I had only previously known in golf.

It is a truism that adversity brings out the best in a person. During my six or seven seasons with Aberdeenshire I had the privilege of meeting many players at their best. This was always especially true of away games where, inevitably, either the quality or the quantity of the team left much to be desired.

I must not leave you with the impression that the Aberdeenshire of the mid-sixties was a disaster area. My memories are of great enjoyment, both on and off the field and, also, of great admiration for the small and enthusiastic nucleus of officials and players who helped provide the continuity from one generation of players to the next.

*

Having been an Anglo-Scot for all eight seasons since leaving school, I now became involved in the Inter District Championship for the first time. After two trials for the North, I was selected as full-back and captain for the North Midlands to play Edinburgh at Murrayfield. Our stand-off that day was a very young Dundonian, Chris Rea, who developed into a very good Scotland and Lions centre and thereafter a respected rugby journalist. However, he was the only stand-off I ever played with who never kicked. Elusive as he undoubtedly was, running every ball he received did not pay off and we lost quite badly. Two weeks later, on the day of President Kennedy's assassination, and this time with me playing a more prosaic game at stand-off, we were much more competitive against the South at Jedburgh, losing narrowly to the only try of the game.

When the teams for the first international trial were announced, I was pleased to be picked at full-back, as opposed to stand-off, with Stewart Wilson from Oxford University as my latest challenger. During the following week I captained, from full-back, a Scottish XV against the Combined Services and in the final trial, Stewart and I were again in direct competition.

Before the team to play France in the opening game of the 1964 Five Nations was announced, Charlie Drummond, now the convenor of the Big Five, very decently, phoned to tell me that I was not selected. I didn't think that I had played particularly badly or that Stewart had played particularly well, but, on reflection, I was pretty sure that Robin Chisholm must have felt much the same way seven years previously when I got my first cap at his expense. If you live by the sword you die by the sword. It was my turn to eat humble pie.

Early in 1964 the All Blacks came to Aberdeen. The team chosen to play at Linksfield included known greats such as Wilson Whineray, Don Clarke and his brother Ian, and an up-and-coming half-back partnership of Earl Kirton and Chris Laidlaw.

With the kick-off timed for 2.15 p.m. at Linksfield, the North Midlands side met for an early lunch in a local hotel. To say that our preparation to play the All Blacks was amateurish would be a huge understatement. In New Zealand in 1959 when the Lions met a Combined Provincial Team it was reputed that they had been having training sessions for at least the previous six months. I was captaining the team from stand-off and having introduced myself to several in the team I had never met, I attempted to lay down some basic tactics. In the line-out, I suggested, that we should jump at three and five, except close to our own line where we would jump at two and four. I turned expectantly to the two second rows to see which one preferred to jump at the front or the middle, only to be told by one of them that he didn't jump because he was usually a prop. Mike Gibb was, fortunately, big for a prop, but it meant a very busy afternoon for his second-row colleague, the athletic Ian Wood, later of oil industry fame. In the event, we punched well above our weight and kept the score down to a 15 points to 3 defeat.

Having missed Scotland's French and New Zealand Tests, I was involved as a travelling reserve for the away games in Cardiff and Dublin and for the Calcutta Cup game at Murrayfield. In the euphoric dressing room after the first win against England since 1950, I could not but spare a thought for Hugh McLeod and Arthur Smith for whom a win over England would have meant so much. With three wins in the Five Nations, losing only to Wales, and a draw with New Zealand, this was the best record of any Scottish side since the Triple Crown winning season of 1938. Stewart Wilson, who I had never seen play before the first trial, had a very successful start to his international career, but I hadn't given up entirely on the hope of making a comeback.

The opportunity came quickly. In May, Scotland had a short, five-game tour to Canada arranged to celebrate the seventy-fifth anniversary of the introduction of rugby to Western Canada, and with Stewart unable to go, having to sit exams in Oxford, I was selected as the only full-back. A typhoid epidemic in Aberdeen very nearly stopped me travelling as it was only at the last minute that I was granted entry to Canada. I had been in Vancouver and Toronto with the Lions in 1959, but the stay in Montreal was a new experience. The rugby was not memorable but I do remember shopping in a supermarket for the first time. It was several years before the first supermarket was opened in Aberdeen.

THIRTEEN

THE END OF THE LINE

I had a very personal reason for wanting to play for Scotland again. In *The Herioter* in my last year at school, George Blamire, our rugby master, wrote that I was arguably the best footballer that the school had produced. Dan Drysdale, with twenty-six caps in the 1920s, held the record for the most caps won by a former pupil and I had stalled on the same number.

By the time of the trials in December 1964 I had had three months of fairly high standard rugby including a game for a Select XV against Oxford University, where, incidentally, Dan Drysdale was one of the selectors, and Stewart Wilson was my opposite number. In the two trials we were again in direct opposition.

It was Stewart's turn to experience second season syndrome when, without any real change in ability from year one when the critics, and that includes selectors as well as the press and the spectating public, tend to magnify the good points, in year two they tend only to see weaknesses.

I felt that I had worked harder for my twenty-seventh Scotland cap than all the others put together and I was looking forward to a fifth visit to Colombes for the opening game of the 1965 Five

Nations. Pace is generally the first thing to go and, in the event, I was too often caught out by a bouncy ball on a hard pitch. We lost 16–8 and I was never picked again. A few weeks later I badly twisted my left knee. An invitation to go to Twickenham as a travelling reserve came too late as I was already in the Aberdeen Royal Infirmary having had the offending cartilage removed by the surgeon, Mr Rennie. I was only twenty-eight years old, which by today's standards is probably when a player is at his peak, but in some ways, it was a relief to accept that my international days were over and that I could now get on with the rest of my life.

As a family we had settled quickly into Aberdeen life with helpful neighbours, work colleagues and rugby and cricket teammates. My school friend Gilbert (Tosh) McIntosh and wife Frances, and Norma, an Atholl Crescent friend of Doreen's, and husband Stewart Hart became close friends. Early on as an escape from redecorating our new house, Tosh and I went to a joinery evening class. We also joined the local squash club and, although I can't imagine how we thought we would find the time to play we joined Cruden Bay Golf Club. For an introductory offer of entry fee and first year's subscription of seven guineas it was too good to miss.

After four summers I stopped playing cricket. At school I had been as keen on cricket as I was on rugby. I think I could have achieved more at cricket but only at the expense of some, if not all, of my three main ambitions on leaving school.

By this time, I was also a member of Royal Aberdeen Golf Club at Balgownie, and golf became my summer sport. The seven hours away from home that it took for a round of golf compared favourably with an away trip to Linlithgow, Stirling, Dunfermline or Alloa to play Scottish counties cricket, so Doreen was happy . . . or maybe just less unhappy?

Eventually I played seven seasons rugby for Aberdeenshire and the North Midlands, retiring in 1969 at the age of thirty-three. By then Alistair had been born, completing our family, and Robin and Iain had started at the excellent local primary, Broomhill School.

I thoroughly enjoyed my rugby in the north. There was great enthusiasm for the game in some unlikely places and I found that the games – while always competitive – were played in a very good spirit. If it was a bit incestuous – I played twelve times against Aberdeen Grammar, and eight times against Aberdeen University, Aberdeen Accies and Dundee High – it certainly cut down on the travelling. I also found that under the influence of a former Scotland scrum-half, Dally Allardice, Dundee High were an attractive team to play against. Oxford University was the only other team I played against eight times, followed by France and England seven times each.

Playing for the North Midlands, I enjoyed the company of old friends David Rollo and Ronnie Glasgow and was encouraged to see young players make the grade through to international level. Ian McCrae was a consistently resilient scrum-half, while the aforementioned Chris Rea, John Frame and Nairn McEwan all cut their teeth in representative rugby with the North Midlands before defecting to either Glasgow or the South.

At club level, Ian Robertson, recently retired from the BBC after fifty years as their radio rugby correspondent, played one season for Aberdeenshire. At that time, he was in his final year at Aberdeen University and was told by his tutor that if he was going to get a degree he would have to concentrate on his work. This meant playing no rugby, wasting no time studying the latest form on the turf and not talking so much. I doubt if anything changed other than the colour of his rugby jersey, but he became a useful attacking addition to the Aberdeenshire team – and he got his degree. I still had one useful contact at Cambridge and armed with that introduction, Ian talked himself into Christ's College and a rugby Blue.

When I stopped playing, I decided to take a complete break from rugby. Instead I became a twelve-month-a-year Saturday afternoon golfer at Balgownie. Since then, I have been a member at Brodick, Goswick and Bruntsfield Links without ever quite being able to match that Saturday afternoon experience at Balgownie.

*

To an incomer, Aberdeen in the 1960s seemed like a large village. The town revolved round the harbour and the fishing industry, although shipbuilding was in decline. Family businesses dominated manufacturing, construction, the professions and the shops on Union Street. Before networking was even a concept, through family marriages and old-school-tie-connections, the heads of these businesses formed a very influential clique in all that went on in commercial Aberdeen. I dipped my toes into the fringes of that group by playing golf at Balgownie and having an end-of-the-working-week refreshment at the University Club.

With Bill Adamson's engineering skills and knowledge of concrete and my background in productivity and planning, the Precast Concrete Company, although small, developed into a profitable part of the Alexander Hall business.

In 1964, we were interested visitors at the Industrialised Building Systems and Components (IBSAC) Exhibition held at the Crystal Palace in London. It was estimated then that there was a demand for a million new homes in the UK and that multi-storey blocks constructed from precast concrete units were one of the quickest and best solutions. Despite the partial collapse of a tower block at Ronan Point in London, this form of high-rise building continued for a generation.

In 1967, six of the major companies in Aberdeen, covering civil engineering, building, precast concrete, plumbing, heating and electrical services and quarrying amalgamated to form Aberdeen Construction Group. Through numerous wholly-owned subsidiary companies the Group traded from the Shetlands in the north to Southampton in the south. The Group's shares were quoted on the London Stock Exchange and its annual results were subject to wider scrutiny. I was employed as part of a small team in the holding company to create a group structure and a system of regular financial reporting. By 1972, the Group was showing a profit of £1.5m on a turnover of £30m and I had been appointed as deputy managing director.

1972, however, was not a good year. Three months of strike action particularly affected the construction sector but also caused power cuts in Aberdeen. The established nucleus of companies within the group were able to minimise the effects but the newer companies, especially those based in the central belt of Scotland were losing heavily. I was delegated by the board to deal with this problem. Realistically, there was no way of achieving a solution commuting from Aberdeen so a move to Edinburgh was essential.

As a family we were enjoying life in Aberdeen. Robin and Iain were doing well at Broomhill Primary and Alistair had started at a nursery. We had redecorated and modernised our house. Doreen had had time to expand her group of friends and had joined Aberdeen Ladies Golf Club. Therefore, I was not popular when I arrived home from work with the news that we were moving to Edinburgh in six weeks. The move was not intended to be permanent but events proved otherwise.

FOURTEEN

RETURNING TO MY ROOTS

Returning to Edinburgh in the summer of 1972 we rented a house in the Murrayfield area for six months while we waited for our new flat at Easter Park to be completed. Near neighbours were Arthur and Judith Smith and family, and Arthur and I soon had a regular, fiercely contested (if low-level standard) squash game. Over the Christmas holidays we also had an enjoyable family kick-about with a football at Roseburn Park.

Robin, at the age of ten was most affected by the move. He had made friends in Aberdeen and was having to start again in a strange environment. Finding a school for the boys was a priority. Because I had led a charmed life at school I had reservations about them following me to Heriot's. However, they had a very friendly and informal interview with the headmaster of the junior school, Gibby Galloway, who had been a mentor of mine both as a rugby master and as an officer in the Scottish Schoolboys Club, which for better or worse allayed my fears.

When I stopped playing rugby in Aberdeen – after fourteen seasons of senior rugby preceded by nine seasons of school rugby – I took a complete break from the game.

Back in Edinburgh three years later, however, with Robin and Iain starting to play rugby for Heriot's at Goldenacre, I gradually got sucked back in. Soon, after watching beginners playing on a Saturday morning, I was refereeing games at that level thanks to the persuasive powers of my former sports master, Donald Hastie. I was also elected onto the Heriot's FP rugby club general committee.

At my very first meeting, it was proposed that the club should go open to the extent of ten per cent of the playing membership. This was strenuously opposed, to the extent of at least one resignation, but I was with the majority who felt that with a new Scottish club national league system due to start the following season (1973/74), we would not be able to maintain our place as a top Scottish club confining ourselves only to former pupils of the school.

This gloomy prediction came close to being immediately realised as, in our last game of the first league season, we had to beat Langholm at Goldenacre to avoid relegation. At half-time, with the score at 18–6 in Langholm's favour, I was working out which grounds I would have to visit to watch the team playing in Division Two the following season. In the end, a win by the nail-bitingly narrow 25–24 margin was enough to see us fight another day.

In the longer term, the decision to overcome eighty years of tradition by becoming an open club has been vindicated to the extent that at the time of writing, Heriot's is the only club not to have been relegated from the top league of Scottish club rugby.

The transition from 1974 into 1975 was seriously marred by the very sad news that Arthur Smith was suffering from cancer, culminating in his death on 3 February. Ever since my first year at Cambridge, I had regarded Arthur as a role model and now that I was back in Edinburgh, he acted as a sounding board for my ideas and problems. It was typical of his character that the last time I visited him at home he was engrossed reading *The Ascent of Man* by Jacob Bronowski. Making use of every minute to the very end.

Under the chairmanship of the Rt Rev Leonard Small, a former moderator of the Church of Scotland, I was part of a group who set up the Arthur Smith Memorial Trust. The trust had the very active support of the Edinburgh Wanderers Rugby Club and included friends and neighbours Fraser Elgin and Alistair Cameron as well as former business colleagues. The trust had broad educational aims, but was also to ensure the continuing education of his three children Jacqueline, Joanna and Ian.

*

The companies within the Aberdeen Construction Group in the central belt were based at Broxburn and Bellshill. They were both all-trades building contractors with an added precast concrete factory at Bellshill. It was immediately obvious that there was considerable scope for savings in senior management and in the office-based functions. The two companies were amalgamated under one management at Broxburn, with Bellshill being retained as a specialist concrete manufacturer. Some staff were offered alternative employment within the Group, but unfortunately others had to be made redundant. Telling someone that they have lost their job is the worst thing I have ever had to do.

One unexpected by-product of the changes was an introduction to sectarianism which I had never experienced previously. After all the shuffling about and with the reorganisation completed, I discovered that one department was staffed entirely by Catholics and another entirely by Protestants. As far as I was aware, it had no influence on the efficiency of the company overall or even the harmony between the two departments, but it was an eye-opener to me.

By the end of 1974, the amalgamated company at Broxburn was still showing a loss. The main ongoing problem was the completion of long-running contracts which had been priced on a fixed cost basis prior to the years of rampant inflation.

I was confident that we now had a good management team in place and there was every reason to believe that we could produce as good a profit as any other business in the Group.

The Group board, however, took a different view. They felt that the central belt companies had been a drain on Group resources for too long and should be wound down. I felt that the board were taking a very short-term position largely to protect their immediate share price rather than looking to the future.

I could have returned to head office in Aberdeen, as I was still deputy managing director of the Group, but as I disagreed in principle with the board's decision and with the family now well-established back in Edinburgh, I decided to resign.

With the help of some creative accounting, Aberdeen Construction Group's annual accounts did not include the losses incurred at Broxburn and I left, with a shell company carrying substantial tax losses.

In the mid 1970s, with the UK joining the European Common Market and, more importantly, with Aberdeen being central to the development of the North Sea oil industry, the Construction Group should have been in pole position to take advantage. For reasons which I have never discovered, the group did not make use of its local knowledge, assets and connections and was eventually bought over by a company based in Yorkshire.

About this time, I had a call from Jeff Butterfield asking if I would be interested in going on an 'oldies' tour, with wives included, to the Caribbean, at some unspecified time in the future, if it could be arranged. Without giving it a lot of thought, and thinking that it would be a nice diversion from looking for work, I said that we would be delighted to be part of the party.

When news came back that the tour was definitely arranged for Easter 1975, my bluff had been well and truly called. Fortunately, I was able to slip into the Heriot's 6th XV and make my comeback at Beveridge Park, Kirkcaldy, behind old friends George Goddard and Hamish More at half-back, and other club stalwarts who eased my way back into the game.

For this short Caribbean tour of only six games in May 1975, Jeff had fortunately assembled as many players as the 1959 Lions had to play their thirty-three matches. As well as Jeff, Dickie Jeeps was also a survivor from 1959, as were Andy Mulligan and Tony O'Reilly, both now resident in the USA and billed to make guest appearances. Hugh Burry, who had played in the back row for the victorious Canterbury XV against the Lions in 1959, was also in the party. Other friends from either Cambridge or Scotland were Calum and Mary Bannerman, Peter and Jill Brown, Frank and Wilma Laidlaw, Brian and Connie Simmers and Geoff Windsor-Lewis. A new friend was David Powell, who reminded me of a Saturday afternoon in 1962 when I was seen disconsolately pushing a pram around the rugby pitch at Long Buckby when I should have been playing in the Middlesex Sevens at Twickenham. David played junior rugby at Long Buckby before progressing to Northampton and England.

Our first stop was Kingston, Jamaica, where we played two games in four days. In retrospect, it is hard to remember how we found time for rugby in the midst of swimming, beach barbecues, cocktail parties and an introduction to reggae music.

On our one free day, a small group, which included Geoff Windsor-Lewis, drove through the Blue Mountains to the beach on the north coast at Dunn's River Falls. It was a unique experience in the hot sunshine to cool off lying in the waterfall. On our return journey we visited Goldeneye – Ian Fleming's estate – where Doreen had the thrill of sitting at the desk where James Bond had been created.

We were hosted in private homes and a feature was their proximity to very basic shanty towns. At night in the house where Doreen and I were staying, metal shutters were brought down to isolate and secure the bedroom area. Driving through Kingston there were areas where it did not seem sensible to stop. I was always apprehensive that our driver might hit one of the many goats on the road and be forced to. On the plus side, it was a pleasure to see the children from these same areas immaculately dressed on their way to school.

One of our games was played on a pitch adjacent to a sugar plantation and the other at the national stadium, built to house the 1966 Commonwealth Games. Both games were won and our only injury was a case of heat stroke suffered by the youngest member of our group, who was somewhat overweight and shall remain nameless.

The pace of life on Grand Cayman was much slower than Kingston but there was no let-up on the round of receptions and cocktail parties. Doreen and I were hosted by the local headmaster and his wife, Peter and Apryl Stokes. As a Welsh couple, they had been hoping to look after Cliff Morgan, but they managed to hide their disappointment and were most hospitable.

We were taken to visit the 'world's first commercial green sea turtle farm' which housed more than 100,000 turtles. The primary purpose was to avoid the near extinction of the species but also to produce a sustainable nutritious food source.

A barbecue was organised for lunchtime at Seven-Mile-Beach, almost as impressive as Luskentyre on Harris in the Outer Hebrides, on the day of the game, and as I wasn't playing, I was able to make the most of the generous hospitality. The ground where the game was played was described as quaint and tiny with liberal sandy patches, and combined with the excessive heat, the locals fancied their chances. However, with Dickie Jeeps giving his usual pugnacious lead, the result was a comfortable victory for the visitors.

Our last stop was on Grand Bahama, where we played our last three games on the same pitch which it was apprehensively noted was full size in both width and length. Overall, the clubhouse, pitch and adjoining swimming pool would have been the envy of a rugby club anywhere in the world.

The standard, too, was higher than we had previously met and we had to work hard to win our final game to edge the series by two games to one.

Our hosts for the week were Ron and Barbara Philip. Ron hailed from St Andrews, where his family had a golf-related business close to the eighteenth green on the Old Course, so we felt quite at home. The highlight of the week was a deep-sea fishing expedition. Doreen, to the manner born, landed three good-sized tuna, while Frank Laidlaw had a seriously long struggle with a dolphin. Even when he got it on board it still had enough power in its tail to give Doreen a memento of the day in the form of a black and blue thigh.

*

Immediately on return from the Caribbean, I started work as a self-employed developer of timber framed houses in association with James Walker (Leith) Ltd. Walkers owned an impressive timber manufacturing factory in Bo'ness and our aim was to break into the local authority housing market.

We immediately got started in a small way with successful developments locally in Edinburgh and East Lothian.

Back at Goldenacre, season 1975/76 was soon underway, and while still refereeing on a Saturday morning, in the afternoons I continued playing with my, more or less, contemporaries, for the 6th XV. I also played occasional midweek games for Edinburgh

Borderers. It was a pleasure to play again with old friends such as Adam Robson and Ronnie Glasgow. In a game against Merchiston Castle School, their scrum-half was a young Roger Baird. In the opposition side of my very first game in senior rugby, at the Kelso Sevens in September 1955, had been Roger Baird senior. They were the only father-son combination that I was ever aware of playing against.

For four years in the late 1970 I received a welcome invitation, and hospitality, from David Chisholm to play at the Greenyards on the Friday evening before the Sevens against a Melrose Junior XV. Regulars in David's Team were Eddie McKeating, Brian Henderson and Jim Telfer as well as the seemingly ageless Ronnie Glasgow and Adam Robson.

The very last game I played was as the committee man travelling with the 3rd XV to play Glasgow Accies at New Anniesland with only fourteen players. I played on the wing, in Kenny Milne's training boots, with my oldest son Robin playing at full-back.

Running a successful 6th XV showed that the rugby club was in good heart. It did, however, have disadvantages. Firstly, no one wanted to be promoted to the 5ths, and more importantly, then as now, it was difficult to get volunteers for the many jobs it takes to run an amateur sports club. I, amongst others, was indulging and hugely enjoying myself by playing rather than helping to run the club.

Consequently, for season 1976/77 I accepted the position as chairman of selectors, for the first three XVs, on the understanding that there would be no formal committee or selection meetings. My thinking was heavily influenced by my experience at Cambridge, where the players had complete charge over everything concerning the actual playing of the game, including selection. It helped that the elected captain was Andy Irvine. Andy already had a stellar international and Lions reputation, which he continued to show on the pitch at

Goldenacre, and overall his enthusiasm and leadership within the club was infectious.

To keep the 2nd and 3rd XVs in the picture, I persuaded as many as possible of my former 6th XV colleagues to take on the responsibilities of team manager, even if only for a month at a time. This had the benefit of keeping a lot of rugby experience active within the club without being too time consuming for any one individual.

Over three seasons, along with coach John Stent, Andy and I tried to establish early-on our best XV and make as few changes as possible week on week. Most Mondays, Andy and I had a quick lunch at the Laughing Duck where we agreed teams for the following weekend. This policy paid off to the extent that we improved over these seasons from 6th to 4th to winning the league in season 1978/79.

When the club went open in the early 1970s, the perceived wisdom was that to stay competitive we would need to recruit forwards to provide the possession to fuel our home-bred backs. In the event, ten of the league-winning team went to the school, including six of the forwards. Dino Steven deserves a mention as being the only player in my experience as a selector who took the trouble to phone me to let me know that he should be playing further up the club. It took him a season or two to back his own opinion, but he became an integral part of that very cohesive pack of forwards.

*

While I thoroughly enjoyed my association with the Walker Group of Companies, and Michael Walker in particular, we never achieved a breakthrough into the local authority housing market. This was at least partly due to the overall decline in the late 70s of the local authority market and also their unwillingness to change from traditional bricks and mortar to the relatively new timber frame construction.

In early 1980, I joined Edinburgh-based blue-chip company, Christian Salvesen. From its origins of whaling in the South Atlantic, the company had diversified mainly into fish processing and refrigerated transport. One of its recent expansions had been the acquisition of a national house-building company, Whelmar Homes. Whelmar had a head office in Leigh, Lancashire with subsidiaries in Northampton, Telford New Town and Linwood, outside Glasgow. My remit was to set up an east of Scotland-based company. Whelmar was in the volume house building market and competed nationally with companies such as Barratts, Wates and Wimpey and locally with Millers and McTaggart and Mickel, amongst others.

Based at head office in East Fettes Avenue, I immediately took over responsibility, from Linwood, for a large development in Aberdeen. With this flying start, I was able to build up the nucleus of a small team comprising a senior site manager, an architect and a quantity surveyor.

Being in head office, I was able to take advantage of lunching in the canteen and meeting people from other departments. One early topic of conversation was the forthcoming first Edinburgh Marathon. Four of us talked ourselves into thinking that it would be a suitable and exciting challenge. Giving ourselves a little over three months to train, we started by running round Inverleith Park after work. My three companions were David Elston, of no known athletic background, but younger than the others, Mike Barrie, a former Watsonian back row forward, and Jim McNeillage, a Commonwealth Games-level badminton and counties-standard tennis player. Jim is still a good friend and a regular golfing partner.

On the big day, we intended to run together but with the numbers involved that proved impossible. In training, I had never run more than a half marathon and on the day I found it very hard going. Running into a strong cold east wind along the exposed stretch from Cramond to Granton was particularly hard and I was surprised just how uplifting it was to get the support of the few hardy spectators. I was happy to finish in just under four hours.

By 1983, the company was profitable on a turnover of over £5 million and had expanded in the Aberdeen area and into Fife. In Edinburgh, we had redeveloped the old Corstorphine Station and for our work at the derelict Portobello Power Station won the top award in Scotland in the National House-Building Council 'Pride in the Job' campaign. It was extremely disappointing to be told less than a year later that Salvesens were pulling out of house building in Scotland. The reason given was that the return on capital employed in housing compared unfavourably with other divisions in the group. It made sense for them, therefore, to invest in these areas.

I was proud of the work we did. The technical team in particular worked wonders in tight inner-city sites and it was hard on them to be made redundant through no fault of their own.

FIFTEEN

THE NEW MAN AT THE CASTLE

In 1984, to mark the twenty-fifth anniversary of the 1959 Lions tour, we held a dinner at the Café Royal in Regent Street, London. It was organised by Jeff Butterfield who, at that time, was running the Rugby Club in Portland Place, London. Out of the thirty-five who appeared in the 1959 team photograph, twenty-seven attended.

Sadly, both Gordon Wood and our tour secretary, Ossie Glasgow, had died and our manager, Alf Wilson, was not fit enough to travel. With Haydn Morgan and Gordon Waddell now living in South Africa that was an enthusiastic response from the rest of the team.

I was particularly pleased to catch up with Phil Horrocks-Taylor who had taught me all I needed to know about work study on a shop floor in Wolverhampton. Not long after I had settled in Aberdeen, I was asked if I was interested in a job in Middlesbrough and, if not, could I recommend someone who might be suitable. Phil had now been working in Middlesbrough for twenty years but was feeling 'bruised'. His career, like mine, had stalled, so we cried in our beer and felt bruised together.

The dinner was planned to coincide with the Middlesex Sevens at Twickenham, which allowed me to take my turn of running the line as Heriot's committee man. I even got a mention from Peter Yarranton, a colleague on the Combined Services visit to the south of France in late 1955 and long-time idiosyncratic announcer on the public address system.

Back home in Scotland, Doreen and I visited Alf Wilson at his home in Dunfermline to pass on the very best wishes from all those who attended the dinner.

*

For most of rest of 1984, I worked on short-term assignments in, amongst others, a hotel in Sandwich, Kent, a laundry in Romford, Essex and breweries in Belfast and Newcastle. Towards the end of the year, Doreen and I went to Fort William to be interviewed for a post with the Outward Bound organisation at Loch Eil. The weather on the day was wet and windy and the accommodation on offer spartan, to put it kindly. It was unfortunate to have to turn down their offer because the work had sounded both worthwhile and interesting.

We had better luck in an interview with the National Trust for Scotland for the position of administrator at either Crathes Castle, west of Aberdeen, or Brodick Castle on the Isle of Arran. With the benefit of Doreen's input, the interview went well and we were offered Brodick. I felt that our previous knowledge of the Aberdeen area might have made Crathes the more likely choice for us, but we were more than happy with the Arran option.

Before making a final decision, we paid a visit to the island with the NTS director for the region, Findlay McQuarrie. On the plus side, our first view of the sun-dappled, snow-clad hills on Arran as we approached the ferry at Ardrossan and our proposed accommodation on the second floor of the castle could not have been more encouraging. This feeling was only slightly offset by the almost deserted appearance of an out-of-season Brodick. The die was cast, however, and in March 1985 I started as the administrator of Brodick Castle, Gardens and Country Park (to give it its full title).

With the start of the season fast approaching, I was both relieved and delighted to realise that I had inherited a well-oiled machine. My predecessor, John Forgie, had left the island in tragic circumstances, but his legacy was such that the new season started without me having to make any decisions or recruit any staff.

Bob and Nancy Bell were live-in custodians. Bob also sold tickets in the entrance hall and Nancy worked in the tearoom. Isobel Miller ran the shop, Anna McCabe appeared as baker of scones, renowned far and wide, and a team of guides arrived, like magic, on their allotted days. The gardens were, as always, kept immaculately by John Basford, who I first met on his return from exhibiting at the Chelsea Flower Show, and his team of five assistants. Derek Warner, our resident ranger, kept a watchful eye on all things concerning the country park.

Being ex-officio on both the Isle of Arran Tourist Board and the Ferry Committee, I quickly had a very useful introduction to the facts of life on the island. Nothing could happen without the ferry service, which was the only connection to the mainland. Tourism was the main source of income on the island and one of the biggest single attractions was the castle.

If these committees consisted of the main movers and shakers on the island, the hoteliers and businessmen, I also soon met the local tradesmen, Willie Inness, the joiner, Ian McNicol, the plumber and Henry Tait, the builder who did regular maintenance work at the castle and surrounding property and who became good friends.

Also, the castle, being the highest building on the island, was regularly used by both the mountain rescue team and the part-time fire service to hone their various techniques and test their equipment.

Soon I was well known throughout the island as 'the new man at the castle'.

The work schedule which I inherited gave me Saturdays free. Never previously having had much time, or inclination, for hill walking, Doreen and I found a new enthusiasm. Although Arran lacks a Munro, Goatfell at 2,866 feet being its highest peak, it is a mecca for hill walkers. Walking directly from the castle, we soon became familiar with circular walks including Beinn Nuis, the A'Chir Ridge, Cir Mhor, the Castles and the Witches' Step which provided wonderful 360-degree views from the Island.

The castle was open for the tourist season from Easter until the end of October. For the first year, my aims were to keep the existing team motivated and to learn the history of Brodick Castle in particular and the Isle of Arran in general.

One of the pleasures of working in the castle was meeting National Trust staff or visitors who were experts in their own field. Preparing for the new season we had a visit from two of the curators from head office, Christopher Hartley and John Batty. This became an annual highlight as they supervised the selection of which of the many silver artefacts in store would be used in new or revised exhibitions at the castle.

On display throughout the castle were a number of paintings on loan from the Royal Scottish Academy. We had an interesting visit from their committee, including president Sir Anthony Wheeler, to check that their paintings were being properly preserved and generally to comment on the quality of the complete collection. The inspection was little more than a formality and the party soon moved on to the summer house overlooking the walled garden where we enjoyed a most convivial lunch.

Alastair Hetherington, the former acclaimed editor of the *Guardian* and then professor of media studies at Stirling University, along with wife Sheila, had a holiday home at High Corrie. As close neighbours on the island they were regular visitors to the castle. They were also generous hosts and stimulating company for a day in the hills. Alastair was very fit for his age and seemed to have perfected a method where he could talk at length without interrupting his progress over the ground.

I spent an interesting morning with a Dutchman who had come all the way from Holland to study in detail a painting hanging on the landing called 'Landscape with Members of the House of Orange returning from Hunting', by Sebastian Vrancx.

On another occasion, I was given a master class on silverware, spending a day with a member of the Schroder merchant banking family. As the owner of a large private collection he was greatly impressed by the range and quality on display at Brodick.

Harry Secombe, who was on the island to record one of his series of *Highway* programmes, visited the castle and his easy manner and Goonish humour soon gathered a crowd. He also found time for a game of golf at Brodick playing with Doreen's clubs.

Of the many old friends who I met as they toured the castle, I was particularly pleased to bump into Eric Evans. Thirty years previously, Eric had captained the English side that I think was the best team I ever played against. We had a long chat and Eric, a blunt Lancastrian, was disinclined to argue against the quality of that team.

The most well-known visitor I had the honour of showing round the castle was astronaut Neil Armstrong. He arrived, without entourage, by helicopter from a holiday at the Turnberry Hotel. With Scottish roots in Langholm he was interested in the history of the area and its buildings and the legend of Robert the Bruce. He then flew out, again without attracting much attention. I got the impression that he was a very private person – the Moon was never mentioned.

Doreen, meanwhile, was not formally employed at the castle, but it was understood that she would 'do the flowers'. At least once a week, a fresh van load was delivered by John Basford, the head gardener. The aim was to present the interior of the castle as a lived-in space so formal floral arrangements were not required. John quickly and expertly demonstrated what was expected and left Doreen to get on with it.

Realising that Doreen was keen on gardening, John set up a plot for her where she grew cabbages, sprouts and potatoes as well as blackcurrants, gooseberries, raspberries and strawberries.

As a variation to our Saturday walks we took part in a charity walk around Arran. Setting off at 7 a.m. from Whiting Bay and walking up the west coast, Doreen managed the thirty-four miles to Lochranza raising £100 for the Lamlash War Memorial Hospital Supporters League. I managed the final twenty-two miles back to Whiting Bay, taking a total of sixteen hours for the round trip. Not having as many friends, I made nothing like as much money for charity as Doreen.

Another Saturday, Doreen acted as my bagman as I ran in the Goatfell Race. The race started in Ormidale Park behind the golf clubhouse in Brodick and involved a distance of just under ten miles and a climb of 2,860 feet. Unbelievably, the record time for the run is just over seventy-two minutes. I just about achieved my target of reaching the top of Goatfell at about the time the leaders were finishing back in Brodick – but that was the easy bit. The power had completely gone from my legs and it took me longer to come down than it did to climb to the top. A good fell-runner is an impressive athlete.

Doreen helped to set up and run a branch of the Save the Children Fund on the island which was very well supported by the local people with their typical generosity.

On the mainland, Doreen had been going to art classes. The husband of one of her walking group had a studio near the castle and Doreen was invited to work with him – not to be taught but to watch and learn. Leslie Marr was a member of the Bomberg School and a very successful painter in his own right. He had a varied background, including Formula One racing driving and photography, spending a season living with the Sami people as he made a documentary film of the reindeer migration in Norwegian Lapland. In London in 1990 we went to view his one-man exhibition at the Cato Gallery in Hampstead.

Quite by chance, we bumped into Leslie and new wife, Maureen, in the cafe at the House of Bruar over twenty years later. I made a throwaway remark saying it was a pity that Doreen hadn't picked up something off the studio floor as a happy memory of her times in his company. Shortly after we got home a package arrived with two paintings and the comment, 'I have over a 1,000 similar in plan chests and am always pleased when something emerges into the daylight.' Needless to say, they now have pride of place in our flat.

Doreen was a regular competitor in the ladies' competitions at Brodick Golf Club, highlights being runner-up in the club championship, being elected vice-captain of the ladies' section and having a unique hole in one. On the short 15th over the Rosa Burn she did a 'Barnes Wallis', the ball skimming the water, running up the bank on to the green and into the hole. The shot was witnessed by walkers on the footbridge as well as her partners.

*

In 1986, Doreen and I were among the 450 guests who attended Tony O'Reilly's 'This Is Your Life'-type fiftieth birthday party at the Killcullen Community Centre, not far from his Irish home, Castlemartin.

We were met by a chauffeur-driven limousine at Dublin airport, which took us to Castlemartin, a Georgian mansion house, where we were to spend the next two nights.

Our accommodation was one of four en-suite bedrooms in a converted stable block now overlooking the swimming pool. We shared the Pool House with old friends Jeff and Barbara Butterfield, Bryn and Betty Meredith and Rhys and Megan Williams.

As well as admiring the quality of the conversion, a walk through the estate showed everything being maintained to the highest possible standard, including the restoration of a 15th century chapel. At that time, Tony was president of Heinz and owner of The Independent Newspaper Group, so his rugby friends were in the minority at the birthday dinner. Among the guests were former Toaiseach Jack Lynch and celebrated Irish poet Ulick O'Connor. Also attending were Paddy Madigan and the Mulcahy twins, Paul and Donal, whom I had played against over thirty years previously as Belvedere College schoolboys. Tony has always been loyal and generous towards his old friends.

Lunch at Castlemartin the following day was exclusively for thirty or more of his old rugby friends with their wives or partners. They ranged from Jackie Kyle, Karl Mullen and Jim McCarthy from Ireland's Triple Crown teams of 1948 and 1949, through to Ireland and Lions colleagues of the 1950s, with Mike Gibson taking the gathering into the 1960s and 70s.

The lunch ended with Cliff Morgan on the piano leading the company through the Lions Song Sheet, finishing with an emotional rendering of 'Now is the Hour'.

As we were not leaving until the following morning, we had dinner with the family. I had been sharing a room with Tony in the Coogee Bay Hotel in Sydney when he first met his wife Susan, so I felt I had been involved right from the start of their relationship.

*

No sooner had the visitors departed Brodick Castle at the end of the season than the locals' interests took over. There were regular concerts held in village halls and at the castle. The local pipe band, brass band and wee swing band were all in great demand along with regulars to the island like Moira Anderson and Peter Morrison. The Gilbert and Sullivan Society produced an annual show and every year there was an inter-village drama competition. There was also an active natural history society holding regular meetings and winter walks.

With so much cultural activity around I was happy to learn that there was also a rugby club on the island. The club had been nurtured by Joe Rae the head PE teacher at Lamlash High School. The facilities were good, with a flat, good-sized pitch and with an adjacent gym for bad-weather training. The fact that they were now playing in a Glasgow and District League concentrated the mind. Fixtures had to be fulfilled, which, taking into account weather and ferry sailings, was not always straightforward.

The players were a mixture of local boys who had finished off their education at a rugby playing-school on the mainland, lads who had come to work on the island with some background in the game and a few recruits from local village football teams. The hotly contested Inter-Village Football League was a summer competition so there were a few talented ball players looking for exercise in the winter.

I enjoyed the four seasons I had as their coach, which was a novel role for me. Despite their general lack of experience the enthusiasm of the players was infectious and the matches were fiercely contested and played in a good spirit. I started off looking for ways to create second phase possession but soon realised that the answer was to fight hard for the first phase and then hang on to the ball for as long as possible. The team had a number of natural leaders, Angus Adamson, now a local Church of Scotland minister, Alistair Dobson, now managing director of a much-expanded Arran Dairies, along with Jimmy Morrison, Ian McDonald, Chris Marryatt and Sid Sillars provided a strong nucleus.

The highlight of the season was the annual sevens tournament which clubs from the mainland, including Heriot's, treated as an overseas tour by staying for the weekend and making their presence felt – not always appreciated by local hoteliers.

One winter, the Royal Scottish Country Dance Society's Annual Ball was held at the castle. To ensure local interest, Joe Rae coached a set comprising his wife Dorothy, David and Clare Hendry, Iain and Moira Small and Doreen and me. We managed a few weeks' practise at the golf club, which allowed us to take part on the big day without looking too out of place. The drawing room in the castle made a perfect setting.

At Hogmanay 1988, we had a house party (delusions of grandeur) at the castle for a group of our son Iain's friends. Our flat was adjacent to two letting flats and we were able to accommodate twelve guests. Iain and wife-to-be Deb from London, Ken and Hazel Middleton and Ian (son of fourth Heriot's international full-back) and Alison Thompson from Edinburgh, Ian and Jeanette MacKenzie from Aberdeen, Andrew and Sarah from London, Peter from Australia and Cindy from New York made up an eclectic group.

The ferry sailing was in doubt all day only arriving at 9.30 p.m. having been diverted from Ardrossan to Gourock. The element of doubt and the fact that the castle was floodlit to welcome them all added to create a romantic slightly fairy-tale impression for our guests.

We dressed formally, the men mainly in the kilt, for a

sumptuous dinner, which by arrangement had been provided by our guests. After champagne at midnight, with Deb at the piano and with most of the boys having a background in the Scottish Schoolboys Club, a sing-song interspersed with action games finished off a memorable evening.

One January, I had the pleasure of attending a Burns Supper at the Bachelors Club in Tarbolton. The property is owned by National Trust for Scotland and open to the public as a Burns Museum so has to be the most authentic possible venue. The principal toast to the Immortal Memory of Robert Burns was skilfully proposed by the Secretary of State for Scotland, George Younger, and the whole evening was wonderfully organised in a formal way.

Another year, Doreen and I went to the Burns Supper held at Brodick Golf Club under the skilled chairmanship of John Sillars, one of the assistant gardeners at the castle. The speeches were outstandingly good and impromptu songs were sung with everyone enjoying a very convivial evening. Of the two events, I suspect that Burns would have preferred the night at the golf club.

After five summers at the castle, we were enjoying life so much on the island that we started looking around for a property to retire to. The criteria were to be near the sea and the hills, with easy access to a golf course and within walking distance for morning rolls and a daily paper.

Nothing we saw on the island quite ticked all our boxes and in any case all our plans for the future were thrown into disarray when I was offered another job.

SIXTEEN

FAMILY MATTERS

When we flew the nest to Arran in 1985, we left the boys Robin twenty-three, Iain twenty-one and Alistair seventeen in Edinburgh. At school, Robin did what I had never done and captained the 1st XV; Iain was a regular 2nd XV player as he moved through the years; and Alistair, after dropping an enormous goal in an early game, decided that he would prefer to play football. At the impressionable age of three or four, Alistair had watched an open-top bus parade as a victorious Aberdeen team returned to town with the Scottish Cup. He has been a regular follower of the Dons ever since and is also a paid-up member of the Tartan Army.

None of the boys showed any interest in, or aptitude for, cricket, although Iain followed in my footsteps by scoring for a season for the Former Pupils 1st XI. Living next door, the boys were all junior members of Bruntsfield Links Golfing Society, and at one point in their late teens, Robin, Iain and I were playing off handicaps of six, seven and eight. There is still a bit of argument about which was which.

During the years we lived in Aberdeen, we went north for our summer holidays. In 1964, we stayed at the Alton Burn

Hotel in Nairn and the next year we ventured even further to the Burghfield Hotel in Dornoch. The hotel was run by brothers Neil (in the kitchen) and Euan (behind the bar) Currie. We all enjoyed ourselves so much that we returned there for the next six years. The atmosphere in the hotel was relaxed and the food plentiful and of high quality. Particularly the first year, the weather could not have been better and the boys enjoyed the beach and sand dunes. Also setting the tone in year one was meeting three families from Aberdeen, the Craigs, the Leiths and the Shepherds. As well as providing me with a four-ball game of golf every morning they were good company for Doreen and the boys on the beach and kept Euan busy behind the bar until the wee small hours.

Over the years I came to really enjoy and appreciate Royal Dornoch as a golf course of outstanding quality. The boys also cut their golfing teeth on the then nine-hole Struie course.

More recently, we have enjoyed golfing holidays at Dornoch with my sister Elsie and husband Niven.

Most recently, at a mixed golf competition at Baberton, as guests of Doreen's brother Brian and wife Joan, we won a voucher, in the sweep, for a four-ball at Dornoch. The boys were all keen to have an opportunity to get back to Dornoch and, with the Burghfield House no longer operating as a hotel, we rented a house overlooking the second green for a week. As well as playing on the championship course, the boys enjoyed playing on the revamped eighteen-hole Struie. It was quite a unique occasion for us having the company of the boys on their own. Alistair's parting remark was, 'Where are we going next year?' So far, we haven't managed a repeat . . .

Robin was slow to settle on leaving school being involved in a variety of entrepreneurial enterprises in Edinburgh, Glasgow and Perthshire before joining us on Arran. At Goldenacre, he was understudy to Andy Irvine but did have one game for the 1st XV.

Iain joined the Clydesdale Bank straight from school and was soon transferred to their St James Street, London branch. He proved to be a late developer by being selected to play full-back for the London United Banks while playing regularly for the Midland Bank.

Alistair, who trained as a hairdresser, was first to marry. He met Gro, a Norwegian girl, in Spain while on holiday with a group of friends from his pub football team. She lived on the small Island of Ormøy, then accessible only by ferry from Stavanger. They were married in March 1989 in the Domkirken Stavanger.

Alistair, now married to Siv, lives on Hundvag, another island off Stavanger. His family now extends to four daughters, Lil Marie, Eva Cathrine, Julie and Mariann, three granddaughters, Emma, Adelia and Marion and a grandson, Loke Emil He worked off shore on a Halliburton well-testing vessel which on one occasion was hijacked by pirates off the coast of Nigeria. Alistair now works in a family industrial plumbing company and Siv as well as being the local accountant for a multi-national company, has become a convert to the game of golf. Their youngest daughter, Mariann, is studying engineering at Trondheim University.

In almost our last act on Arran, Iain married Deb, an Essex girl he met at the Midland Bank rugby club in Beckenham, at the local church in Brodick. The reception was held in a marquee in the grounds of the castle with the excellent catering supplied by Iain and Jane Mcfadzean of the Brodick Bar. Deb is half Scottish with a father, Jim Barbour, from Sorn in Ayrshire, who moved south to join the Metropolitan Police. When she met Ian, Deb was working as a steel trader but after son Calum was born she retrained as a school teacher.

Iain, meanwhile, changed from retail to investment banking. After working in the City for a number of years, he moved to a company based in Sevenoaks, not far from their home near Bromley. Currently, they are working together in the Dordogne in France where Deb is headmistress of an off-shoot of a girl's boarding school in the south of England, with Iain acting as bursar. Calum has now graduated in French and German from Nottingham University and is working in Leeds in sports broadcasting.

In 1998, nine years after his brothers, Robin, our eldest, married Hilde at Gyland Kirke, not far from Flekkefjord in Norway. He went to visit Alistair in Stavanger, met Hilde, who was then working as a nursery school teacher, and more or less never came back. They have settled in Hilde's home town of Flekkefjord, where Robin, until recently, was involved in off-shore salmon farming. I was impressed that he was able to present a paper to a managers' meeting in Norwegian. He is now working in on-shore turbot farming. They have two sons – Oscar, who is at Stavanger University studying to be a primary school teacher, and Carsten, who is still at school, soon to be an apprentice electrician. There is a rugby club in Flekkefjord where Robin and Carsten both go to training. Carsten plays occasionally and has been on courses to qualify as a referee in both union and league.

It may be tempting providence, but Doreen and I feel that the boys have ended up with wives who have been good for them.

We have also been very lucky with all the in-laws. Jarl and Biorg on Ormoy, Jim and Beryl in Romford, Kare and Signe in Stavanger and 'Bestefar' in Flekkefjord. They have all been welcoming and generous in their hospitality.

Like all our family, we do not see enough of them.

To celebrate our Golden Wedding in 2011, we had a family week, including four granddaughters, three grandsons, one great-granddaughter and one great-grandson at Brodick, where we have so many happy memories. Apart from golf with the boys at both Shiskine and Brodick, the highlight was a family climb of Goatfell. Rather like the Grand Old Duke of York, I imagined leading them all to the top of the hill. In the event, Oscar age eleven and Carsten age nine set a pace which no one else could match. This undoubtedly showed the benefit of the very steep climb which was part of their daily walk to school in Flekkefjord.

SEVENTEEN

PAXTON HOUSE

The challenge, and the attraction, of moving to Paxton was to be responsible for opening the house and grounds to the public for the first time. With a lead-in time of two-and-a-half years, my experience in both the building industry and the visitor attraction market at Brodick would be used and tested to the full.

The estate was now owned and being managed by the Paxton Trust, having been generously handed over by the last in the line of previous family owners, John and Catherine Home Robertson.

The chairman of the Paxton Trust was Sir Kenneth Alexander, an academic economist who had recently retired as Principal of Stirling University. Previously he had been a non-executive director of Upper Clyde Shipbuilders and Chairman of the Highlands and Islands Development Board. I had met him socially at Alistair Hetherington's cottage in High Corrie and it was he who asked if I would consider a move across country to Berwickshire.

Other trustees were Kathleen Dalyell – wife of Tam of the Binns, whom I had previously met as my father had been her father's clerk – Alistair Rowan, Principal of the Edinburgh College of Art, Herbert Coutts, Edinburgh Council's City curator, George Miller, a local farmer in Northumberland, Allan Swan, a local architect, and former owner John Home Robertson, then MP for East Lothian.

Paxton House, situated on the north bank of the River Tweed roughly three miles upriver from Berwick, is a classical neo-Palladian country house designed by John and James Adam and built in the 1750s for the Homes of Wedderburn. The Adam influence is carried on internally with plasterwork features and an extensive collection of Chippendale furniture. In the early 19th century, a large picture gallery was added to the east to house the family collection and was furnished with neo-classical furniture by Trotter of Edinburgh.

The budget for the restoration of around £2 million was funded largely by the National Heritage Memorial Fund. Ian Begg, noted for his work on historic buildings, was appointed architect. Wren and Bell, who I had worked with previously, were structural engineers, and the professional team was completed by Jim Murphy as quantity surveyor. Virtually all the work would be carried out by specialist sub-contractors.

As well as the serious structural restoration required in the picture gallery and restoration of all the finishes in the main house, the provision of car parking, shop, tea room and toilets were all essential.

Exciting early news was that the picture gallery, once restored, would become an outstation of the National Galleries of Scotland.

In restoration work no detail is too small. After extensive investigation by experts in their own fields colour schemes were established throughout, period wallpapers reproduced as required and an oil cloth floor covering for the entrance hall was commissioned.

There were over 1,000 visitors when Paxton opened its doors to the public over Easter Weekend 1992. Ian Begg had redesigned the stable courtyard into an atmospheric visitor centre with all the necessary modern facilities. There were still details to finish but an extensive display of daffodils throughout the grounds presented a mature and timeless setting.

The picture gallery too had been restored and by 4 June, the day of the official opening by Princess Alexandra, the National Gallery had completed their hanging.

Tommy and Anne Patterson, who lived in the East Lodge at the entrance to Paxton House, were the first and most helpful people we met. Without their knowledge of the local area it would have been much more difficult to build a team to make the project work. To open daily for six months, we needed to recruit at least twelve staff to cover tearoom, shop and guiding.

We lived in a comfortable apartment in the west wing, with a bedroom door opening into a small enclosed garden. Until opening day, however, it was like living on the fringe of a building site. Our escape in Berwickshire was not to the hills, as on Arran, but to the coast. We discovered many enjoyable walks in the St Abbs, Coldingham, and Eyemouth area. The sandy beaches south of the border in the area around Holy Island and Bamburgh could also be exhilarating. There was also always something of interest to see walking in the historic town of Berwick-upon-Tweed.

One lunchtime, with Doreen out golfing, I went home for something to eat. As soon as I opened the door I realised that the upstairs was on fire. A quick response from the fire brigade managed to confine the worst of the fire to the kitchen where it was discovered that a faulty refrigerator had been the cause. We were able to sleep downstairs but had nowhere to prepare food. A clause in our insurance policy allowed us to eat out one meal daily. For over six weeks we were able to compare what was on offer in different restaurants and pubs over a wide area.

On Arran, I was lucky if I saw a rugby match every two weeks, but now I was spoiled for choice. I joined Kelso, who for the previous two seasons had been Scottish club champions, and also the local club in Berwick. Every Saturday morning, I had a choice to make. As well as Kelso and Berwick I also enjoyed watching an Armstrong brothers-inspired Jedforest and Duns was always a pleasant ground to visit.

I had never previously watched a Border League game. As a city player, I had always believed that Border teams reserved an especially physical game to play against us. Nothing could have been further from the truth. In the Border League, no quarter was given – and none asked. The games were good to watch and played in a fine spirit but it is a hardy breed who play regularly in the Scottish Borders.

Berwick rugby club, like the football equivalent, have their ground in England but play in the Scottish leagues. The original club had been disbanded during the Second World War and in the early 1990s were over twenty years into their second coming. They were well-organised and ambitious, with good playing pitches and a modern clubhouse at Scremerston on the southern outskirts of the town. Having thrown out my boots on leaving Arran I had to invest in a new pair when I was drawn in by their enthusiasm to help out with the under-13 squad and, from time to time, with the 1st XV backs.

After five years as next-door neighbours, the Scotland/Home Robertson relationship, which had never been much more than polite, had deteriorated to the decidedly frigid. It was not a comfortable situation and I was happy to accept an early retirement package and return to our flat in Edinburgh.

EIGHTEEN

THE CALL OF GOLDENACRE

Returning to Edinburgh with an almost new pair of boots, I was soon back involved at Goldenacre. I worked for three seasons with the 2nd XV, who were in a very competitive league playing a good standard of rugby. It was a good mixture of mature players happy to share their experience and youngsters keen to learn and push for a game for the 1sts.

In the mid 90s, Heriot's went through a lean spell. In season 1996/97 we were bottom of the league and only avoided relegation by the number of teams being increased for the following season. The next year it was a decidedly nervous group of supporters who headed to the neutral ground of Pennypit in Prestonpans for a play-off decider against Kelso, the runners-up in Division Two. A hard fought 33–12 win guaranteed at least another year in the top flight.

Successive club presidents agonised over the possibility of relegation happening during their period in office. When I took my turn early in the 2000s I was saved sleepless nights, as by then, we were competing at the other end of the table. Like all my predecessors, after four years as vice and president I was elected an honorary vice president.

2001 marked the centenary of the school moving its playing fields from a ground near the Water of Leith, known as Warriston, Logie Green or Puddochy, to the present site at Goldenacre. The governors of the George Heriot's Trust decided to celebrate the occasion by building a new pavilion and I was extremely flattered when it was opened as the K J F Scotland Pavilion. It is hard to put into words just how much that meant to me. I doubt if it was possible for anyone in their school years at Heriot's to have spent more time than I did at Goldenacre. It brought to mind all the support and encouragement I had received along the way ranging from William McLachlan Dewar, the headmaster, through teachers Gibby Galloway, an early mentor, rugby master George Blamire and cricket master Lindsay L Mitchell, to the groundsmen, Arthur Creber, Alec Gillies and Henry Drummond who, to begin with, kept putting me out of the ground, but ended up as great supporters. I was also aware of how much pleasure the honour would have given to my mother and father.

Historically, honorary presidents of the rugby club were headmasters of the school, presidents of the Scottish Rugby Union or Lord Provosts of the City of Edinburgh. This tradition was broken by the election of Wallace Deas as the senior serving 'Club Rugby Man' in 2000. In 2005, David Edwards took over that position and I was greatly honoured to be elected as their successor as an honorary president of the club in 2007.

*

In the bigger picture, in 1995, Scottish rugby had been dragged kicking and screaming into the professional era and there was a serious split between the SRU and some of the clubs and also some of the senior players on how professionalism should be introduced organised and funded.

I represented Heriot's on the Premier League Forum for six years at this interesting time. The forum, then as now, had no powers. How their proposals would be financed was not discussed but there was a strong lobby who would have supported our four districts being represented by Glasgow Hawks, Melrose, Watsonians and either Stirling County or Dundee High. Organisationally, Glasgow Hawks, under the leadership of Brian Simmers, were ahead of the other clubs and I think they were only a year or two away from being the present Glasgow Warriors. How to finance the operation was their only real stumbling block.

The SRU pre-empted further discussion by, I think, rushing into giving professional contracts to 135 players covering our traditional four districts. At that time, there was no immediate prospect of full-time fixture lists and it was unfair to the players who were being asked to choose between their careers outside rugby and a very uncertain future in the game.

It was only after six years, in 2001, when our four professional teams had been reduced to two and a viable fixture list with Welsh and Irish districts and a European Cup was created that professional rugby began to feel established in Scotland.

Ian McGeechan and Jim Telfer were the main driving forces in Scottish rugby throughout this period of transition. Jim, I thought, was spot on in thinking that professional rugby in Scotland could only prosper if it attracted support from beyond its traditional following. On the Premier League Forum, Heriot's were largely supportive of what they were doing, except when it came to the re-establishment of a third professional team based in Galashiels. In many ways the Borders, as the heartland of Scottish rugby deserved to be represented but I felt then, as I still think now, that the SRU had neither the finance nor the depth of talent to justify another team.

What has been a success has been the marketing of professional rugby with Glasgow and Scotland consistently playing to full houses and, hopefully, Edinburgh will follow suit once they settle into their new purpose-built ground on the back pitches at Murrayfield.

*

In late June 2007, we received a very nice invitation from Tony O'Reilly to join him in Paris in October for three nights, including tickets for the World Cup final. His intention was to organise a party for as many players from the Lions tours of 1950, 1955 and 1959 who could make it to Paris.

We accepted immediately and, with time to spare, we decided to take the opportunity of spending a week in Paris, Wednesday to Wednesday, with a three-day break over the weekend to join the party.

Doreen had previously been in Paris twice, once as a schoolgirl and once as a teacher leading a party, and I had played rugby there ten times but we had previously only spent two nights in Paris together. Twenty-five years previously, we had broken our journey from the Dordogne back to Calais so we had a lot of sightseeing still to do.

When we booked our apartment for the week, it sounded good. With an address just off the Champs-Élysées, at the L'Arc de Triomphe end, and with views of the Eiffel Tower it was ideally situated. In fact, however, it was very ordinary, with the toilet across a wide common landing, the shower being hand-held in a tiny cubicle and, by standing on a chair, we could just get a glimpse of the top of the Eiffel Tower. We could only be wryly amused comparing it to the luxury to come at the five-star Hôtel Plaza Athénée.

In all, thirty Lions had accepted Tony's invitation. We arrived resplendent in made-to-measure Lions dress blazers, courtesy of

Peter Kininmonth, who should have been with us but who very sadly and unexpectedly died after all the arrangements had been made.

Peter's absence limited the number of 1950 tourists to four. Bleddyn Williams and Jack Matthews a legendary Welsh centre combination, Jim McCarthy, Irish wing-forward of 1948 and 1949 Triple Crowns fame, and Jackie Kyle, one of the best stand-offs of all time – and, of course, my schoolboy hero.

There were twelve players from 1955 who toured in South Africa, including Dickie Jeeps, Hugh McLeod, Bryn Meredith and Tony O'Reilly, who were also part of the 1959 team in Australia and New Zealand. Another fourteen from 1959 made the total up to thirty.

Accommodation was split between the Hôtel Plaza Athénée and the Hotel Bristol with the two official dinners for the whole party being held at the Plaza Athénée. The atmosphere throughout was relaxed and informal and no expense was spared. Tony and his second wife Chryss were gracious and generous hosts.

While the ladies watched the final on TV in our hotel, the men were whisked off in chauffeur-driven limousines to the Stade de France to see England play South Africa. As a relatively neutral spectator, it was a disappointing game to watch with South Africa's five penalties beating England's three. After the game, it was straight back to the hotel, where it was nearly midnight before we joined the ladies for dinner.

Left to our own devices, Doreen and I did a lot of sightseeing. Doreen took me to the Montmartre area where she had had her portrait painted by a street artist on her trip as a teacher in 1960, and I showed her the Hotel Normandie where the Scotland XV always stayed. The Normandie is at the bottom end of the Avenue de L'Opéra and close to the Louvre. We admired the new glass pyramid structure in the courtyard, but the length of the queues put us off making a visit to the gallery. We moved on through the Tuileries Gardens (where, on a Cambridge tour, we had had a short training session) to the Jeu de Paume. On our previous visit to Paris, we had seen an exhibition of Impressionist paintings in this small but impressive gallery.

With two days still to go, and Doreen's pedometer being overworked, we used the Batobus on the Seine to take some of the strain. Setting off both days from the Eiffel Tower, we went the length of the route to the Ile St Louis, exploring both sides of the river there and working our way back.

In the Marais District, as well as the Pompidou Centre, we visited the Musée Carnavalet a converted mansion housing a fascinating exhibition illustrating the history of Paris.

Crossing the river via the Île de la Cité, we took time to visit Notre-Dame before lunching on the other side in Boulevard St Michel, part of the Student Quarter. We had a walk in the Jardins de Luxembourg before a stop on our return journey at the Musée d'Orsay, the converted terminus station of the Paris-Orleans line.

To round off our stay in Paris in spectacular style, on our last trip on the Seine it was getting dark and many of the buildings were floodlit with sparkling lights moving up and down the Eiffel Tower. It was a wonderful end to a wonderful week and another thanks must be paid to my great old friend, Tony, for making it happen.

*

Two years later, the 1959 Lions got together once again to celebrate a remarkable fifty years since our great expedition. As with the twenty-five-year reunion, this was a team members-only occasion. It was organised for us by the Mike Burton Events

Company and we entered the professional era by having our weekend generate a modicum of sponsorship.

The main event was a dinner held at the East India and Sports Club on the Friday evening, followed on the Saturday by a visit to Twickenham to watch England play the All Blacks.

It was appropriate that fifteen of us enjoyed our 'last hurrah' and the team we fielded was: Ken Scotland, John Young, David Hewitt, Phil Horrocks-Taylor, Niall Brophy, Bev Risman, Dickie Jeeps, Hugh McLeod, Ronnie Dawson, Syd Millar, Roddy Evans; Bill Mulcahy, Bryn Meredith, Ken Smith and Noel Murphy

Only two were 'playing' out of position, which, of course, we were used to, and also without the benefit of a bench of substitutes.

We were all very relaxed in each other's company. Over the past fifty years, we had played rugby with or against each other and met as individuals or in groups at various events, so the chat and banter resumed immediately and continued non-stop with everyone joining in.

Individual and team memories of fifty years ago were given another airing, which all led to a further strengthening of the bonds of friendship and respect which we had built up in our round the world trip in 1959.

For those of us lucky enough to be there, it was a very happy couple of days but the toast to absent friends was particularly poignant.

*

In November 2010, I was delighted to be involved in the SRU's inaugural Hall of Fame dinner, which was held at Murrayfield under the chairmanship of Ian McLauchlan, the reigning SRU president, with the BBC's Dougie Donnelly acting as MC.

The Big Five selectors on this occasion, who had the daunting task of distilling over 100 years of Scottish rugby and over 1,000 international players into a team of twelve, were John Beattie, Ian McGeechan, Norman Mair and Chris Rea under the chairmanship of John Jeffrey.

The outcome of their lengthy discussions was:

David Bedell-Sivright	Pre World War One
G P S Macpherson	Between the Wars
Ken Scotland	1945-1959
Sandy Carmichael	1960s
Andy Irvine	1970s
Finlay Calder	1980s
Gavin Hastings	1990s by public vote
Ned Haig	Instigator of seven-a-side rugby
Bill McLaren	The Voice of Rugby
Ian McGeechan	Coach and player
Jim Telfer	Coach and player
Gordon Brown	Triple British Lion

I was obviously very, very flattered to be picked out of the short list of six in consideration for the immediate post-war slot. As a schoolboy I had cheered as Douglas Elliot made life a misery for opposing stand-offs and had been in awe of Peter Kininmonth's drop goal against Wales in 1951, but the other three I had played with and admired greatly.

Jim Greenwood was the captain when I was first capped in 1957. He made his reputation as a player on the 1955 Lions tour to South Africa and went on to become a natural leader and an innovative thinker about the game.

Of the thirty-two international matches I played for Scotland and the Lions, Hugh McLeod was a teammate in twenty-seven. Hugh played all six Tests on the 1959 tour to Australia and New Zealand and played forty successive games for Scotland, then a record, from 1954, before retiring at the end of 1962. He was the ultimate all-round prop forward.

Arthur Smith, as I have already written, became a role model for me during my time at Cambridge and later in Edinburgh we became close friends. It was heart-breaking to see his life cut short at the early age of forty-three.

Hugh McLeod and Douglas Elliot were subsequently inducted in 2013 and 2017 respectively.

Two years after this wonderful evening, at a ceremony held at the National Museum of Scotland in November 2012, and attended by Doreen and our three boys and wives – Robin and Hilde, Iain and Deb and Alistair and Siw – I was inducted into the Scottish Sports Hall of Fame.

Starting in 2002, eighty-seven sportsmen and sportswomen, covering thirty different sports had already been inducted. Football was most heavily represented with fourteen, followed by athletics and rugby union with nine each. Swimming eight, golf seven, boxing six and Formula 1 with four were the next most honoured sports.

Added to the Roll of Honour on the night was Rhona Martin who was skip of the Great Britain curling team which won the gold medal at the Winter Olympic Games in Salt Lake City in 2002. This was a first for curling.

There were two additions to the list of swimmers: Belle Moore who won a gold medal at Stockholm in 1912 and is still the only Scottish female swimmer to have won Olympic gold; and Margaret McEleny who represented Great Britain at four Paralympic Games between 1992 and 2004 winning three gold medals out of a total haul of fifteen.

Willie Anderson was born in North Berwick and emigrated to the United States at the age of sixteen to make his living as a golf professional. By the time he died at the early age of thirty-one he had won the US Open four times between 1901 and 1905.

I joined the following rugby players already included:

K G McLeod
G P S Macpherson
Eric Liddell (cited primarily as an athlete)
R Wilson Shaw
W I D Elliot
Andy Irvine
Finlay Calder
Gavin Hastings
David Sole.

It was a very relaxed and pleasant family occasion made even more special for Alistair who got the opportunity to speak to Archie Gemmill, of 1978 football World Cup fame, who was a fellow inductee. His outstanding goal against the Netherlands was sadly one of very few memorable moments for Scottish supporters. Standing beside Archie gave me the unusual illusion of being a big robust rugby player.

NINETEEN

THE EVOLUTION OF THE GAME

In the aftermath of the 111 lines-out epic against Wales at Murrayfield in 1963, I was invited by my retired English teacher, Charles S Broadwood, to write an article for the *University of Edinburgh Journal* which he was then editing. Charlie was the doyen of Heriot's rugby. In the 1920s he had played scrum-half in an unofficial championship-winning team and in the 1930s the school 1st XV had five unbeaten seasons while he was master in charge. The subtext to this invitation was obviously to explain what the modern players had done to ruin his 1920-30s vision of the game. I think it makes interesting reading all these years later to consider how the game was changing in those days, and how it has evolved – almost constantly – ever since, and so reproduce it below:

'Well-nigh everything that there is to be said about the game of (rugby) football has already appeared in print.' As this quotation is taken from a book written by Harry Vassell, published in 1898, it is with diffidence that even these few words are added. Rugby football, however, has changed a great deal since the days of

Harry Vassell, and especially in a season when the introduction of new laws are artificially changing the game still further it is interesting to attempt to trace the development of the game up to the present day.

The vast majority of players, and spectators too, accept the game as it is played in their time without questioning how it arrived in its existing form. It is only when there are major alterations in the laws that the game as such comes under scrutiny. The student then finds himself faced with the philosopher's problem of whether the game is progressing towards some ultimate perfection or whether it is now in an advanced stage of degeneration.

The history of rugby football shows how the game has evolved and points to the conclusion that it must continue to evolve to survive under contemporary conditions. No law or aspect of the game can be considered sacrosanct. This is not an argument that change should be made solely for the sake of change but rather to emphasise that any popularity rugby football has in the present day is due to the changes that have taken place over the years. It is not too much to say that the original game of rugby-football would have practically no appeal in 1965. Not all the changes, however, have been the result of long thought out plans to improve the game either as a player or a spectator sport. Indeed, the vital change, for example, of reducing the numbers on each side from twenty to fifteen players, about 1875, happened for no more logical reason than that harassed secretaries were finding great difficulty in raising the full complement of twenty players.

It is the evolution of rugby-football and the tactical approach used, so necessary to understand the game in its present form, that will be traced in this article.

For the sake of convenience, the development of rugby football can be divided into the following four periods: pre-1880, 1880–1905, 1905–50 and post-1950. These divisions are not clear cut in any sense, partly because the changes have been gradual, and partly because the game did not, and still does not, develop simultaneously in all rugby-playing countries. An obvious example of this divergence of ideas occurred in the Scotland v Wales game of 1893. At this time the positioning of the fifteen players in each team was still the subject of local whim. Wales had by then adopted the now recognised positions whereas Scotland played with nine forwards and six backs, a circumstance which resulted in a heavy defeat for Scotland and a hasty adoption by them of the new positioning. No example in the modern game could show quite so obviously this trend but it suffices to say that the possibility does still exist.

Rugby football in the pre-1880 period bears little or no resemblance to modern rugby. Although William Webb Ellis made history in 1823 by picking up the ball and running with it, there was in this era about as much open play and running with the ball as one would expect to see in the Eton Wall game. Of the forty players on the field twenty-eight were forwards and their main mode of attack was to kick, or hack, the ball forward and past their opposite numbers. They did not heel the ball. Consequently, the backs on either side had to rely on the random hacking of the opposing forwards to gain possession, and when they did, it was the man with the ball against the entire opposition. A writer of those days stated that, 'backs have to make their own chances and fight their own way — nobody makes openings for his neighbour'. He also wrote that, 'to chuck before being held suggests funk'. This type of game might have appealed to the diehard 'feet-Scotland-feet' supporter but it completely lacked cohesion of any sort.

During the years around 1880, rugby football began to take the form that would be recognisable to the modern spectator. The number of players by then had been reduced to fifteen a side and the forwards to nine or ten. With fewer players on the field the idea of lateral passing among the backs was introduced and this was followed by the forwards heeling the ball to give their backs the possession they required to indulge in handling movements. With these two innovations the modern game was born. It is interesting to note that the Scottish schools, particularly Loretto, and to a lesser extent Fettes, Merchiston and Edinburgh Academy, were among the first teams to experiment with and indeed to introduce the novelties of this period.

If the years pre-1880 were dominated by the forwards with their interminable mauls and hacking, and the years round about 1880 were years of transition to the new handling game, the last years of the old, and the first years of the new century were the high-water mark of back play unhampered by undue interference from the forwards. The forwards became mere purveyors of the ball to the backs who now played the more decisive part in winning a match. It is curious to realise that despite all that has happened since, this formula is still widely held to be the game of rugby football. It is also the great weakness even now of much forward play in all classes of the game.

The 1905 season was dominated by the very successful All Blacks touring team from New Zealand who were responsible for much of the increase in popularity of the game about this time and also for the infusion of many new ideas. As well as having a back division to match the best in Britain they brought with them the then new concept of aggressive forward play based on intensive backing up of the man with the ball, with all fifteen players capable of taking part in a concerted handling movement. Their other main innovation, for better or for worse, was to introduce into rugby football a dedication of both mind and body which had hitherto been lacking. From this point onwards the aspiring player has had to get fit to play rugby rather than to play rugby to get fit.

The years spanning both world wars although mainly dominated by vintage back play also showed a growing appreciation of the necessity for the forwards to provide some sort of preliminary diversion prior to letting their backs have the ball. In general terms it is probable that during this period there was a more even balance between forwards and backs than at any other stage in the game's history. This on the surface would appear to have been the logical conclusion of the development of the game and it should have been played for evermore under these conditions.

What has happened since 1950, however, has spoilt this happy ending and has raised the problem of finding an equilibrium between forwards and backs. In both a positive and negative sense, the last decade has seen the re-emergence of the forwards as the dominating force in rugby football. Where they have been used as an extra attacking force, as the French forwards were in the late 1950s under Lucien Mias, they have added another dimension to the game. Unfortunately, where a team has failed to exploit their forwards' supremacy or where neither side has been able to assert any forward supremacy, the game has had a tendency to bog itself down in an excess of set pieces and a corresponding lack of loose and fluid play.

To discover why the game has evolved past what was thought in the 1920s and 1930s to be its final form, it is necessary to consider the differences in tactics between these years and the 1950s and 1960s.

The main arguments laid against the game in the years 1950-64 were that sides went on to the field determined not to lose rather than determined to win, that the wing forwards had too much potential destructive power and that the back division of the defending team adopted a wholly defensive position. These very points, however, have been cropping up in rugby literature in isolation and together since the late nineteenth century, and conversation with players of the pre-war era confirms that many of the ills in today's game were also common then. If this was so, why was it found necessary in 1964 to make radical changes in the laws in an attempt to make it more difficult for one side to dominate a match with purely negative and defensive tactics?

Specialisation, which has had an influence in most aspects of our modern society, has played the decisive role in what to many lay followers and critics, both professional and amateur, has been the downfall of rugby football. The practical expression of specialisation has been to limit severely the element of doubt as to which side will gain possession of the ball from the set pieces. This has led to the side not expecting to obtain the ball to adopt an uncompromisingly defensive set-up. For the receiving back division to pass the ball in such circumstances was not so much an indication that they wanted to live dangerously as that they wanted to give enormous advantage to the opposition. It is not possible in an article of this length to go into great detail, particularly of a technical nature. The final outcome, however, of these tactics was that in a match where there was anything at all at stake it became virtually impossible to start a handling movement directly from a scrummage or a line-out.

Specialisation among the forwards was not unknown, of course, in the 1920s and 1930s but there was still then a decided element of 'first up, first down' in the scrummages, and even in post-war days the desired loose head was contested. This concept of forward play was casual in the extreme, compared with that brought to a pitch of perfection by the 1951 Springboks. Danie Craven, who was the coach travelling with this team, in his book, *On Rugby*, goes into the duties of the individual forward with an almost unbelievable attention to detail. Indeed, his book explores the art of scrummaging with a scientific thoroughness normally considered to exist in sport only to explain the perfect golf swing.

How then should the game be played and viewed in the 1960s? The idea that rugby football is a game where the forwards exist purely to ply their backs with the ball and that these backs by slick handling can create a situation for one of their number to race majestically up the wing to score a try is a conception that dies hard. The fact that this 'ideal' game probably never existed is irrelevant because it is what was thought to exist that sets the pattern. If it ever did exist, it has gone, perhaps not forever for who can say how the wheel may turn again, but it is certainly not of today's game.

Rugby football today, and of the immediate future, depends not on scoring direct from scrummages and line-outs but of using this first possession to create a situation from which possession is again obtained. This can go on indefinitely until the normal organised defensive structure of the opposition is weakened and the creation of the all-important extra man in the attack is secured. Rugby football played to this pattern will produce a game of infinite variety in which all members of a team will have the opportunity to take an active, creative and crucial part. The skilful handling of the French forwards, the bulldozing handling rushes of the All Blacks and the Springboks, the fire and fury of the Irish with the ball at their feet, and the traditional wheel and take of Scottish packs will all have their vital part. Indeed, they must play their part because it is the forwards' vital role, by using as wide a variety of methods as possible, to produce the second phase, and subsequent possession which eventually makes scoring a try in a closely contested game a feasible proposition. This pattern too will produce more concerted back play than has been possible in recent years because more attention is being paid to giving them 'good possession' rather than all possession.

Times have changed, and rugby football has changed a great deal too, since its origin in 1823. What has to be realised is that what was possible in the context of the 1920s and 1930s is now no longer possible. It is to be hoped, therefore, that the new laws, introduced this season, will not be looked upon as a means of turning the clock back thirty or forty years, but instead will stimulate the thoughts of everyone connected with the game towards this new pattern of play more fitted to our own day and age, and perhaps to the great and glorious days that lie ahead.

My current thinking

Rugby is essentially a contrived game which, unless you are brought up in the faith, is difficult to understand and enjoy. When I played, it was considered very much a players' game. We played because we enjoyed it and providing entertainment for the spectators may have been a side effect but was certainly not high on our list of priorities. In most games, winning was top of the list.

Now that international rugby union is part of the entertainment events business, I will try to bring my thoughts on the evolution of the game up to date.

To entertain, the ball must be kept in play, with few stoppages and with the scoring of a try suitably rewarded. In the 1960s, the value of a try was increased to four points and subsequently to its present five points. Apart from the reduction of the value of a drop goal from four points to three points early in my career, the value of kicks at goal has remained constant.

Arguably place-kicking has now become easier and is overvalued. When I started in school rugby, the ball could only be placed on the ground, usually by the scrum-half, when the kicker started his run up to the ball. When this was relaxed, the kicker would then directly place the ball on a tee of mud prepared by the heel of his boot. Both these options were more or less impossible on a dry, hard pitch. For a while at big games, the kicker would be brought a pail of sand to allow him to build a tee for the ball. Now, of course, all place kicks are taken off the individual's personal tee. Adding to that, the variable condition of the old leather ball compared to the modern more constant composition ball, would suggest that taking a point off the value of place kicks at goal would be a more realistic comparative reward.

The most immediately successful of the 1960s changes to create more space, was the redefining of the offside line. Until then at a scrum, as long as you were behind the ball you were onside. Now the offside line is five metres behind the back foot of your own scrum. Then, at a line-out, the offside line was down the middle of the forwards right across the pitch. Now it is ten metres back for both teams.

This definite improvement has been partly eroded by allowing lifting in the line-out and bending the law requiring a straight put-in down the middle of the tunnel at a scrum. As a result, it is seldom now that a ball is won against the head and defences are set up and waiting accordingly.

Another successful change in that era designed to keep the ball in play was originally introduced as the 'Australian Dispensation'. This discouraged kicking the ball out of play on the full outside your own twenty-five-yard line (as it was known then). Tactical kicking mainly from the half-backs has needed to become more precise. However, the old adage that a good kick puts the opposition under pressure and a poor kick puts your own side under pressure hasn't changed. That hasn't, however, discouraged a lot of purely speculative kicking in the modern game.

With the outcome from scrums and lines-out largely preordained, the main area of contest for possession is now the immediate aftermath of a tackle. For long after it had been written out of the laws, Norman Mair – in my opinion one of the great thinkers about the game of his generation – hankered after the return of playing the ball with the foot after a tackle before it could be handled. That solution is unlikely to be considered any time soon, but the present laws must be a nightmare to referee even with qualified touch judges and video assistance.

The introduction of substitutes for injured players in the late 1960s was the only other major change in the laws on the path towards World Cups and professional rugby union.

The last three decades of the 20th century (up to the confusion caused by professionalism in 1995) will, I think, be considered as a highpoint of the amateur game comparable with the 1920s and 30s.

For spectators at Murrayfield watching matches in the Five Nations, the average points scored per game rose from sixteen in the 1950s and 60s to twenty-seven in the 70s and thirty-one in the 80s. Evidence that the law changes had been both necessary and successful.

The introduction of domestic league and cup competitions throughout Europe with coaches now taking a leading role, provided a focus for both players and spectators. In Scotland, it shook up the comfortable status quo and gave opportunities to ambitious, previously little-known, clubs to climb up the league structure, the outstanding examples being Currie and Stirling County.

With Grand Slam wins in 1984 and 1990, Scottish rugby was in good heart. In 1984, only twenty players were involved and nineteen had learned their rugby in Scotland. Of the sixteen who played in 1990, ten had learned their game in Scotland. It is also interesting to note how few substitutes were used in that decade.

Scotland also had a successful finish to the 20th century by winning the last Five Nations Championship in 1999. It was a sign of the changes in the immediate aftermath of the game going professional that although eleven of the team had learned their rugby in Scotland, only two of them, Gordon Bulloch and Cammy Murray, were then playing for a Scottish club.

It is now coming up to 200 years since William Webb Ellis first picked up the ball and ran, and to keep the game's current popularity another rethink is overdue. It is easier to state the problems than to find solutions.

Rugby has always been a hard, physical game, and there is now less foul play than previously, but it is now beyond physical – it is brutal. At least part of that problem is due to the game no longer being for thirty players but now for forty-six and scrums have been reduced to a time-wasting farce being orchestrated by the referee. While it was once the object to create space with two or three phases of play, endless phases with minimal movement only add to the brutality.

When I was playing at Leicester in the early 1960s and finding space on the pitch a problem, Phil Horrocks-Taylor suggested that, as the pitches were not going to get bigger, it would be necessary to reduce the number of players in each team. As this smacked too much of rugby league it was never a possibility to be taken seriously.

In 2016, when Bev Risman, who had an outstanding career in both union and league, published his autobiography, he concluded with a chapter called 'The New Rugby'. In it, he envisaged the two codes becoming one. With both having entrenched financial interests, I think that unlikely, but union could solve at least some of its problems by turning to league for some inspiration. With pitches now in lavish purpose-built stadia even less likely to get any bigger, the reduction in the number of players in each team to thirteen makes a lot of sense. The scrum is already de-powered and reducing the number of forwards from eight to six will do away with the pretence that there is any serious competition for possession. With players and, perhaps more to the point, coaches moving readily across codes, it will become evident that the need for sheer bulk will be much reduced. Quick possession would then be the primary object when awarded a scrum.

The other most obvious innovation from league would be a to put a limit on the number of phases one side could retain the ball. Six, as allowed in league, would seem adequate.

The two main distinctions between the codes would be the line-out and the competition for possession after the tackle.

Given time to settle in, even with the welfare of the players high on the agenda, I think the necessity to have specialist substitutes would be much reduced. Three or four versatile players should be able to cover most eventualities.

How would those changes affect the amateur club game in Scotland, which is closest to my heart? The straight answer to that is probably not at all. The problems now are finding the dedicated volunteers necessary to run our clubs, the lack of numbers playing the game and the interface between the professional and amateur games. With most youngsters now being introduced to the game through mini rugby at their local rugby club, it is the cumulative ambition of these clubs that keeps the Scottish game alive.

TWENTY

AND NOW THERE IS ONLY GOLF

I remember in my early teens walking to a cricket practice with Ronnie Bateman, with whom I also played rugby and tennis, and agreeing that if we could be really good at any sport we would choose golf because of the length of time it was possible to keep playing.

Sadly for Ronnie, neither of these wishes came true as he died tragically young, ironically at Lothianburn after a round of golf.

For me, although I have never been really good, at least half my boyhood fantasy has come true as I am still enjoying regular fairly competitive golf.

A previously unconsidered benefit with golf is the handicapping system. It is surprising how many games involving players of varying ages and handicaps go to the last putt on the eighteenth green.

My father was a member of the Royal Burgess golf club at Barnton and I had lessons from the professional there, H B Watt. The grip and stance were ingrained at a young age. This was still wartime because I remember the course was reduced to fourteen holes – the present thirteenth to sixteenth being ploughed up.

Living on the north side of Edinburgh, getting to either of the only two corporation courses open at that time at the Braids or Carrick Knowe by tram, carrying even a half set of cut-down clubs was a major exercise. As a result, my early golf was more or less confined to our family fortnight's holiday. Usually with my brother Ronnie, we went round and round the nine hole ladies' course at Lundin Links, for several years, followed by Alnmouth, the Burnside at Carnoustie, for two years, Cullen, Prestwick St. Ninians, a course long since lost under a housing development, Llandudno and the Eden at St Andrews.

At Carnoustie I kept my score against level sixes and at Prestwick, aged fourteen I broke 100 and then 90 for the first time. Not exactly an infant prodigy then. The next step of breaking 80 was a long time coming and was not something I ever managed with any regularity. Although, now into my eighties, I have twice beaten my age in a medal, off the forward tees.

During my time in the army, at Cambridge and for two years working in the English Midlands, I played very little golf. In New Zealand in 1959, however, I did manage to fit in twenty rounds – mostly in a Scotland v England challenge with Gordon Waddell against Bev Risman and Bill Patterson. In Auckland, I also played with Terry McLean, the leading local rugby writer, and Gibby Abercrombie, a Heriot's and Scotland hooker then working locally as a GP.

It wasn't until I was living in Aberdeen in 1965 and close to stopping playing both cricket and rugby that I joined Cruden Bay golf club. For the first time I handed in two cards and was given an official handicap of seventeen. Five years later, having totally abandoned both cricket and rugby, I was playing regular all-year-round golf at Royal Aberdeen and had reduced my handicap to six.

The timing could not have been better because I had been invited to represent the Rugby International Golfing Society in the Sean Connery Invitation Pro/Am golf tournament at Troon on the understanding that my handicap was no higher than six.

The thirty-six-hole tournament was held the weekend before the 1970 Open at St Andrews and attracted a host of top professionals including Bob Charles, Bobby Locke, Arnold Palmer, Peter Thomson and Lee Trevino.

There were twenty-five three-balls playing and my partners were Kel Nagle, the 1960 Open champion at St Andrews, and Dick Smith, the 1958 Scottish amateur champion and Walker Cup player, and a member at neighbouring Prestwick. Gordon Masson, a golfing friend from Aberdeen and a future president of the Scottish Rugby Union, kindly acted as my caddie.

There was not much to choose between my partners. Neither was a long hitter, but they were accurate, consistent, pragmatic and very easy and encouraging company to play with. None of our scoring was remarkable but Dick and I did win a minor prize for joint amateurs.

As I was already a country member at Bruntsfield Links Golfing Society when we returned to Edinburgh in 1972, I was able to jump the long waiting list and get regular golf. The combination of the change from links to parkland golf and a re-introduction to the rugby scene saw my handicap quickly go up to twelve. It never came back down six but I did play off single figures for another thirty years.

With the boys growing up, Doreen, who had originally been well coached by David Houston at the Braids, supplemented by Ian Smith at Hazelhead, was finding more time for golf. We had played a few mixed foursomes before we left Aberdeen and we now became regulars on the Lothians circuit. We had a few early successes but as Doreen's handicap dropped so did our success level.

My old school friend, Eddie McKeating, was now living in Glasgow and had met up with an old Royal High School opponent, Tom Bottomley. Back in Edinburgh I had similarly met up with Jimmy Jarvis. We were all members of different clubs, East Renfrewshire and Kirkhill in Glasgow and the Burgess and Bruntsfield in Edinburgh, and a new intercity cross-school rivalry was started.

After a few years, and with all our wives now playing golf, this challenge was extended to an annual weekend away which continued for over twenty years. Our first few years were based at Stranraer but as we all moved home over the years we based ourselves variously at Bamburgh, the Dormie House at Foxton Hall and Matfen Hall in Northumberland, and Drumoig, Gifford, Melrose and Powfoot in Scotland.

As a couple, we helped form a local mixed group called the Equinox, comprising six couples who played a round robin over the summer. Apart from expanding our group of friends it proved a good way of getting games on a variety of different courses. As the group expanded over the years the format changed to an annual outing. After over thirty years it was decided to retire the group while there were just about enough members left to form a quorum.

Another way of getting competitive golf on different courses was through attending outings and playing in competitions with the Heriot's FP golf club. Playing with my brother Ronnie, we won the foursomes in 1975 and 1977 and I won the singles in 1981.

Over the years, I have had a lot of pleasure playing in outings of the Rugby International Golfing Society (RIGS). When I first became eligible, the Scottish Section had an annual well-attended weekend outing at Old Prestwick. It was fascinating to discuss rugby with people like Herbert Waddell, Max Simmers and Laurie Duff, who had played all their rugby before the war. When I took over as secretary of the Scottish Section from Hamish Dawson in the early 1970s, the outing had been reduced to one day, alternating between Glasgow and Edinburgh. Every new cap was invited to join the RIGS at a life membership of £1.00, but numbers steadily decreased until the outing was abandoned.

To compensate for the lack of an outing an annual match against a team of former Scottish golf internationals was held, alternating between Old Prestwick and Muirfield. Playing off current handicaps, the games were usually close and definitely competitive. It was noticeable that hitting a bad shot affected the golfers more than the rugby players. The last match was held at Prestwick in 2015, the golfers winning by 7–1, with the following teams:

RIGS	SUGS
David Bell	David Carrick
Peter Brown	Gavin Lawrie
Pat Burnet	Alistair Low
David Johnston	Scott MacDonald
Euan Kennedy	Keith MacIntosh
Ken Scotland	Neil MacRae
Derek Stark	Fraser McCluskey
Donald White	John McTear

In 2004, I drove down with Brian Neill to a RIGS Four Home Unions outing at Royal Liverpool golf club at Hoylake in the Wirral. Apart from the opportunity to play on an Open Championship course, it was most notable for meeting Bev Risman for the first time since he had left rugby union to play rugby league. We had played a lot of golf together in New Zealand and we subsequently arranged games at Penrith, where he was a member, Auchterarder, where he and Ann had a time-share, and at Bruntsfield.

In 2013, Doreen and I planned a holiday in Ireland round a RIGS Four Home Unions outing at Lahinch. As well as catching up with the Rismans, we enjoyed meeting a number of contemporaries including Budge Rogers, Stewart Wilson and Roger Michaelson. Off the back tees this was a very tough test for a mixed bag of recreational golfers. To compensate, the Irish more than lived up to their reputation for hospitality.

Unlike the RIGS, the British Rugby Club of Paris (Scottish Section) goes from strength to strength. Founded in the 1920s to give moral support to the 'parent club' it is now purely a social group running two golf outings yearly, currently at Luffness and Gullane No. 2, and an annual dinner. There is a maximum limit of forty-five ordinary members and the only qualification is to have played rugby and be a member of a golf club. The family names of Carmichael, Duff, Hastings, McClung and Paterson Brown echo through the generations.

Now that I am retired, I play regularly at Bruntsfield with two groups. On Wednesdays I play with the Amblers. They were started in the early 1990s by two retired doctors, John Loudon and Bruce Scott, and grew fairly quickly into an Association of Medics, Bankers, Lawyers and others. There are now twenty-five playing and six dining members with regular attendances of twelve or more for an 8.15 a.m. draw all now expertly organised and controlled by Ian McLeod.

On Tuesdays, I play with the aptly named Tuesday Group under the benign presidency of Tony Nixon with a more leisurely 9 a.m. start. At our peak we had fourteen members. Half were past captains of Bruntsfield, half were also members at Muirfield and half were Watsonians. There were others, like myself, who didn't fit any of the above.

*

The first of my three ambitions which I achieved was playing rugby for Scotland. Long since the smell of liniment remains but a distant memory, I still watch a lot of rugby. The professional game is something that I mainly watch on television; being a creature of habit, however, I still feel that winter Saturday afternoons are for spectating at a live rugby match and so if Heriot's are playing in Edinburgh, I will retrace my steps to Goldenacre or to their opponent's local ground. If Heriot's are playing beyond the city limits, I like to choose the most attractive-looking club fixture in north Edinburgh. Edinburgh Accies at Raeburn Place, Stewart's Melville at Inverleith and Royal High at Barnton are all within walking distance of home so I get a bit of exercise as well as the opportunity to see a good cross section of the Scottish club scene.

For the actual participants in these games, the players, the referees and touch judges, the harassed committee people and the gaggle of committed spectators, their enjoyment seems much as I experienced playing at a variety of levels in the 1950s and 60s.

If I can see any moral to draw from my winter Saturday afternoons, it is that participation in amateur team sports should be very actively encouraged in our increasingly specialised and materialistic world.

Sic transit gloria, which I translate as 'fame is short-lived', is showing off that I passed a Latin exam – my second ambition – which allowed me to enjoy three wonderful years at Cambridge.

When I was living and working in Aberdeen and dropped by Scotland for the third and final time, I was happy that I had had my day in the sun and that I could get on with the rest of my life. It just never occurred to me that I might be remembered all these years later – and so thank you for taking the time to read this book.

Last but not least, sixty-six years after I struck gold with Doreen, at the George Heriot's School Easter dance, I can reflect that achieving my third ambition, our marriage, now fifty-nine years ago, was undoubtedly the most important of all. Through good times, and occasionally not so good, Doreen has been a constant source of strength, common sense and loving support. At the latest count, our family now totals three sons, three daughters-in-law, seven grandchildren and four great-grandchildren. Our only regret is that they are so far from us and we wish we could be together more often.

AFTERWORD

During the course of going through old clippings while putting this book together, I found the following article from my old teammate, Chris Rea, which appeared in the *Independent* in December 1999. I would like to thank him for his kind words.

The master of all trades: Ken Scotland

It helps when our boyhood heroes have heroic names. Even before I had seen him, K J F Scotland had a fan. My first sighting of him was from the Murrayfield terraces in 1957 on the foulest of days. Scotland were playing Ireland and 10 minutes before the kick-off a blizzard reduced spectating to a battle for survival. No matter, I stuck it out to the bitter end, if only to make sure that my man would come through unscathed. He looked so pale and frail one feared for his life.

Scotland was a magnificent footballer, blessed with exquisite balance and such natural skill he could play anywhere in the back division. On the 1959 British Lions tour to the Antipodes he occupied every position behind the scrum except wing, and starred in all of them. The New Zealand writer T P McLean perfectly captured him when he wrote: 'He floated like summer down through the New Zealand defence.'

Although he began his rugby life at school as a stand-off, and despite the fact that he occasionally occupied that position at the highest levels, it was as a full-back that his reputation was made. His versatility was not restricted to the rugby field either. He was a first-class wicketkeeper, playing once for Scotland, an opportunity which he claimed he conspicuously failed to take with both hands. He played off a golf handicap of six and three years ago he won the Scottish Rugby Union pro-am over the formidable Dalmahoy course with a gross 73.

If Scotland was not the original running full-back he certainly lifted the art to new heights through his instinctive awareness of time and space. From nowhere he would materialise between the outside centre and wing and with such stealth that opposing defences were almost invariably caught unawares. Slight of build and tipping the scales at no more than 11st, Scotland was, nevertheless, a robust defender, employing his uncanny sense of position and his speed into the tackle to great effect.

Seldom do we get closer to our heroes than mere worship, but on an autumn Saturday in 1963, fresh out of school, I found myself in opposition to my idol, playing for the Scottish Midlands against the North of Scotland in a district trial.

Scotland was by then getting to the end of his career, although he was still the country's first choice full-back, despite the fact that he was playing his rugby with the least fashionable of the leading clubs.

On this occasion Scotland was playing stand-off and, occupying the same position, I had the comforting presence alongside me of Ronnie Glasgow, a deadly assassin of a flanker and the scourge of opposition half-backs, particularly if they were French or famous.

Scotland most definitely fell into the latter category, and when he took up his position behind the scrum almost within touching distance of our back row, Glasgow began pawing the ground in anticipation of the carnage. But it was Scotland who was the destroyer. Not once during that game, I swear, did either Glasgow or I lay as much as a finger on Scotland, whose mastery of angles and deception was out of this world.

Scotland could never be accused of self-advancement and never by a word or deed did he seek to benefit from his talent. But those who truly knew their rugby understood his sublime skills. Tom Kiernan considered him to be the finest full-back he had played against and that redoubtable Welshman and scribe Vivian Jenkins, who could genuinely claim to be in the vanguard of running full-backs as early as the 30s, believed him to be the best player in Britain.

The style, elegance and sportsmanship with which he played his rugby are the precepts by which he lives his life, combined with an enduring modesty and a wonderfully dry wit. A newcomer to the district side came over to introduce himself. 'I'm Arsol Rhind,' he said a little nervously. 'Well, Arsol,' replied Ken, slightly taken aback but ever anxious to please, 'it's my belief that every good team needs one.'

APPENDIX I

PLAYING RECORD

Team	55/56	56/57	57/58	58/59	59/60	60/61
Royal Signals Catterick	12	10				
Northern Command	3	5				
Officers Training Wing, Royal Signals	3					
1 Training Regt. Royal Signals	8	10				
Royal Corps of Signals	2					
Army	8	5				
Combined Services	1					
Heriot's	3		3	5	4	4
SRU Trials	2	2	1	3	1	2
Army North		1				
Scotland		4	1	4	4	5
Heriot's XVs		2				
Invitation XVs			2	1	3	1
Edinburgh			1			
Trinity College, Cambridge			8	1	2	
Cambridge University LX Club			8			
London Scottish			1	1	4	
Cambridge University			7	24	12	17
Co-Optimists			1		1	
Barbarians			3	2		1
Territorial Army				1		
Scotland/Ireland					1	
Scottish XV						1
Harlequins					1	
British & Irish Lions					22	
Ballymena						6
Lurgan						1
Leicester						
Aberdeenshire						
North of Scotland						
North & Midlands						
Highland						
Buchan						
Edinburgh University Wednesday Club						
Total	**42**	**39**	**36**	**42**	**51**	**42**
Sevens Tournaments	4	6	1		5	1

61/62	62/63	63/64	64/65	65/66	66/67	67/68	68/69	Total
								22
								8
								3
								18
								2
								13
								1
	2		1			1		23
2	4	2	2	1				22
								1
4	4		1					27
1								3
4		1	3	2	4	2		23
								1
								11
								8
				2				8
								60
								2
3	1							10
								1
								1
		5	1					7
								1
								22
								6
								1
24	16							40
	2	15	13	17	15	16	11	89
		2	3	2		3	1	11
		4	3	3	7	3	3	23
			1					1
				1				1
						1		1
38	**29**	**29**	**28**	**28**	**27**	**25**	**15**	**471**
	3	2		3	1	1	1	30

BRITISH & IRISH LIONS TOUR FIXTURES 1959

Date	Opposition	Location	Selected	Injured	Score	Points
Sat 23 May 23	Victoria	Melbourne	FB		53–18	1t
Sat30 May 30	New South Wales	Sydney			14–18	
Tues2 June	Queensland	Brisbane	FB		39–11	2t
Sat 6 June	AUSTRALIA	Brisbane	FB		17–6	1dg
Tues 9 June	NSW Country XV	Tamworth			27–14	
Sat 13June	AUSTRALIA	Sydney	FB		24–3	1p 1c
Sat 20 June	Hawke's Bay	Napier	FB		52–12	3t
Wed 24 June	Poverty Bay-East Coast	Gisborne			23–14	
Sat 27 June	Auckland	Auckland	FB		15–10	
Wed 1 July	NZ Universities	Christchurch	FB capt		25–13	1p 2c
Sat 4 July	Otago	Dunedin	FB capt		8–26	1c
Wed 8 July	Combined XV	Timaru			21–11	
Sat 11 July	Southland	Invercargill	SO		11–6	2dg
Sat 18 July	NEW ZEALAND	Dunedin	FB		17–18	
Wed 22 July	West Coast-Buller	Greymouth			58–3	
Sat 25 July	Canterbury	Christchurch	FB		14–20	1dg
Wed 29 July	Combined XV	Blenheim		*	64–5	
Sat 1 Aug	Wellington	Wellington	FB		21–6	
Wed 5 Aug	Wanganui	Wanganui			9–6	
Sat 8 Aug	Taranaki	New Plymouth	FB		15–3	1dg 1p
Tues 11 Aug	Manawatu-Horowhenua	Palmerston North	FB		26–6	
Sat 15 Aug	NEW ZEALAND	Wellington		*	8–11	
Wed 19 Aug	King Country-Counties	Taumarunui		*	25–5	
Sat 22 Aug	Waikato	Hamilton		*	14–0	
Wed 25 Aug	Wairarapa-Bush	Masterton	FB		37–11	
Sat 29Aug	NEW ZEALAND	Christchurch	FB		8–22	
Wed 2 Sept	NZ Juniors	Wellington	SH		29–9	
Sat 5 Sept	NZ Maori	Auckland	SH		12–6	
Wed 9 Sept	Thames Valley-Bay of Plenty	Rotorua	FB		26–24	2t
Sat 12 Sept	North Auckland	Whangarei	C		35–13	2t
Sat 19 Sept	NEW ZEALAND	Auckland	C		9–6	
Sat 26 Sept	British Columbia	Vancouver			16–11	
Tues 29 Sept	Eastern Canada	Toronto	FB		70–6	2t 2c

Played 33, Won 27, Lost 6, For 842, Against 353

Personal record: Played 22, Won 18, Lost 4, 12 tries, 5 drop goals, 6 conversions, 3 penalties: 72 points

When Allan Massie published his excellent book, *A Portrait of Scottish Rugby*, he selected a Scotland XV from 1951 – when he had first become a spectator – to 1984, when the book was published, which was as follows:

Andy Irvine

Arthur Smith
Jim Renwick
Ken Scotland
Roger Baird

John Rutherford
Roy Laidlaw

Hugh McLeod
Colin Deans
Sandy Carmichael
Gordon Brown
Alastair McHarg
Douglas Elliot
Jim Telfer
David Leslie

APPENDIX IV

Scottish Rugby Magazine's all-time Scottish rugby greats XV
(1964-1994):

Ken Scotland

Andy Irvine
Scott Hastings
Ian McGeechan
Keith Robertson

John Rutherford
Gary Armstrong

David Sole
Colin Deans
Iain Milne
Andy Reed
Gordon Brown
John Jeffrey
Finlay Calder (captain)
Iain Paxton

APPENDIX V

Leicester Tigers' team of the twentieth century:

Ken Scotland	1961-62	Scotland
Alastair Smallwood	1920-25	England
Clive Woodward	1979-85	England
Paul Dodge	1975-93	England
Rory Underwood	1983-97	England
Les Cusworth	1978-90	England
Bernard Gadney	1929-39	England
Bob Stirling	1948-53	England
Peter Wheeler	1969-85	England
Darren Garforth	1991-2003	England
Martin Johnson	1989-2005	England
George Beamish	1924-33	Ireland
Doug Prentice	1923-31	England
Dean Richards	1982-97	England
Neil Back	1990-2005	England

APPENDIX VI

Ballymena RFC Millennium XV. Flattering as it was to be included in this team, I actually never played full-back for Ballymena. In the six games I did play, all were at stand-off. At scrum-half in all these games was Jonny Moffett, who played for Ireland that season. In the pack there was a promising youngster by the name of Willie John McBride and a seasoned prop destined to become president of the IRB, amongst many other honours, Syd Millar.

Ken Scotland

Trevor Ringland
Wallace McMaster
Ian McIlrath
Jimmy Topping

G Jamieson
Jonny Moffett

PA Millar
Steve Smith
Syd Millar
Willie John McBride
Ian Dick
Harry Steele
Brian Robinson
Gordon Hamilton

APPENDIX VII

Putting together a select XV from my Scotland contemporaries took quite a bit of thought.

I played more games with Arthur Smith and Hugh McLeod than anyone else and they would be automatic selections on the right wing and loose head prop respectively.

The nucleus of the pack would be from seasons 1961 and 1962, with Norman Bruce and Dave Rollo joining Hugh in the front row. In the second row, my selection Frans ten Bos and Mike Campbell-Lammerton would have competition from Hamish Kemp, who was an excellent jumper in the line out. As ever, back row selection is fiendishly difficult. John Douglas, Ronnie Glasgow, Ken Ross and Ken Smith made up the back-row in those two seasons, but how can you overlook the talents of Jim Greenwood and Adam Robson? In the end I plumped for a combination of Ronnie, Jim and Ken Smith.

Gordon Waddell would play stand-off and the other wing three-quarter would be Ronnie Thomson in a close call with Ian Swan and Ronnie Cowan.

I coincided with five very good scrum-halves with different strengths. Stan Coughtrie, Arthur Dorward, Alec Hastie, Tremayne Rodd and Brian Shillinglaw would all have a claim but whose style most suited Gordon would get the nod.

I always felt that centre three-quarter was the most difficult position on the field to play really well and that was mirrored by the number of different combinations produced by the selectors. I have narrowed the choice down to three, Iain Laughland, Eddie McKeating and George Stevenson.

I would have been more than happy to make up the team with the following:

Ken Scotland

Arthur Smith
Eddie McKeating
Iain Laughland
Ronnie Thomson

Gordon Waddell
Stan Coughtrie

Hugh McLeod
Norman Bruce
Dave Rollo
Mike Campbell-Lamerton
Frans ten Bos
Ken Smith
Jim Greenwood (Captain)
Ronnie Glasgow

INDEX